THE INCREDIBLE PHILADELPHIA PHILLIES TRIVIA BOOK

THE INCREDIBLE PHILADELPHIA PHILLIES TRIVIA BOOK

300 QUESTIONS FOR THE SUPER-FAN

KEVIN REAVY
AND
RYAN SPAEDER

Sports Publishing books may be purchased in bulk at special discounts for sales promotion, corporate gifts, fund-raising, or educational purposes. Special editions can also be created to specifications. For details, contact the Special Sales Department, Sports Publishing, 307 Fifth Avenue, 4th Floor, New York, NY 10016 or sportspubbooks@skyhorsepublishing.com.

Sports Publishing® is a registered trademark of Skyhorse Publishing, Inc.®, a Delaware corporation.

Visit our website at www.sportspubbooks.com.

10 9 8 7 6 5 4 3 2 1

Library of Congress Cataloging-in-Publication Data is available on file.

Cover design by David Ter-Avaneysan
Cover photos credit: Getty Images

Print ISBN: 978-1-68358-538-1
Ebook ISBN: 978-1-68358-539-8

Printed in the United States of America

This book was fun to write. We had help and inspiration from a wide array of people and resources:

Erik Seybold was immensely helpful with research and editing. Jason Katzman and the crew at Skyhorse are the best in the business. Baseball-Reference.com and, of course, the Phillies, were incredible resources. The best Toms in the baseball—McCarthy and Burgoyne—always an inspiration.

Contents

Introduction

The Phillies were born in 1883—one year prior to the invention of the fountain pen, the Linotype typesetter, and the very first espresso machine: three items that played critical roles (directly or ancestrally) in this book finding a spot on bookshelves and toilet tanks by 2026. Incidentally, the modern toilet mechanisms we know today were also invented in the 1880s . . . by a Brit named Thomas Crapper. Soldiers returning to the US from World War I had gotten used to seeing the name plastered on latrines overseas, and that's why we still call a toilet "the crapper" today.

If you think that opening bit of trivia stinks, we've got good news—the rest of the book is nothing but Phillies facts and fun. There might be some toilet humor here and there, but it's mostly raw, unique trivia to challenge (and hone) your fanhood of Philadelphia's Fightin' Phils.

We wrote *Incredible Baseball Stats I & II* in 2017/19, one of the first book series to make analytics palatable to SABR-sensitive stomachs. Our intention was to use statistics to uplift some of the most incredible stories in baseball history. Our goal is similar with this book.

We packed *The Incredible Philadelphia Phillies Trivia Book* with 300 questions that highlight some of the coolest moments, players, and personalities of the team's storied, sometimes crappy, history.

Let's get this one out of the way first:

How many championships have the Phillies won?

Two. Just two. After almost 150 years.

Luckily, that unfortunate historical record has not stopped the Phillies Phaithful from being the best, loudest fans in all of Major League Baseball. Win or lose, it's always entertaining. We hope you have a similar experience with this collection of Phillies trivia.

GOIN' DEEP: 100 QUESTIONS & INCREDIBLE STORIES

QUESTIONS

Ryan Spaeder has made a career out of digging through stats to uncover fantastic baseball tales. Test your knowledge and learn the stories behind these incredible players and moments.

1. Which Phillies player is the only player in team history to hit a walk-off home run on the same date in consecutive seasons?
   A. Jayson Werth
   B. Carlos Ruiz
   C. Cody Asche
   D. Larry Bowa
   Answer on page 29.

2. Which Phillies player is the only player in team history to hit at least 20 home runs in each of his first two big-league seasons?
   A. Darin Ruf
   B. Tommy Joseph
   C. Cameron Rupp
   D. Cody Asche
   Answer on page 29.

3. Which Phillies catcher became the first ever to hit a home run, steal a base, and throw out a runner in a game?
A. Cameron Rupp
B. J. T. Realmuto
C. Darren Daulton
D. Carlos Ruiz
Answer on page 29.

4. Which Phillies player holds the National League record for most consecutive games without being caught stealing?
A. Jimmy Rollins
B. Pat Burrell
C. Tony Taylor
D. Pete Rose
Answer on page 30.

5. Which Phillies pitcher is responsible for the only loss Jake Arrieta suffered during his remarkable 31-start stretch from 2015 to 2016?
A. Aaron Nola
B. Cliff Lee
C. Roy Halladay
D. Cole Hamels
Answer on page 30.

6. Which Phillies player hit four home runs in a game and later in his career abandoned his team while on a bender, got kicked off of a train for a drunken brawl, then died going over Niagara Falls.
A. Ed Delahanty
B. Chuck Klein
C. Mike Schmidt
D. Kyle Schwarber
Answer on page 30.

7. The Phillies moved out of the hitter-friendly confines of the Baker Bowl, which measured just 280 feet to right field and 300 to the rightfield power gap, in June of 1938. Which Phillie has led the franchise in batting average since (minimum 1,000 plate appearances)?
A. Bobby Abreu
B. Chuck Klein
C. John Kruk
D. Jim Eisenreich
Answer on page 31.

8. Which batter has had the fewest plate appearances per home run during their time with the Phillies?
A. Kyle Schwarber
B. Ryan Howard
C. Jim Thome
D. Mike Schmidt
Answer on page 31.

9. This Phillies pitcher became the first pitcher to have at least 200 strikeouts and fewer than 30 walks in a season since Cy Young in 1904 *(hint: this season inspired one of this book's authors to flood Twitter with baseball stats):*
A. Curt Schilling
B. Cliff Lee
C. Roy Halladay
D. Aaron Nola
Answer on page 31.

10. This Phillies pitcher is the only in franchise history to record a strikeout for each of the nine first outs of a game—and would go on to make it 11 of 12:

A. Aaron Nola
B. Roy Halladay
C. Steve Carlton
D. Curt Schilling

Answer on page 31.

11. How many three-ball counts did Roy Halladay have during his perfect game—toying with the possibility of losing it on a free pass?

A. Zero
B. One
C. Two
D. Three or more

Answer on page 31.

12. Four players ever have amassed 20 doubles, 20 triples, 20 home runs, and 20 stolen bases in a season—Frank Schulte (1911), Willie Mays (1957), Curtis Granderson (2007), and which Phillie?

A. Juan Samuel
B. Dick Allen
C. Garry Maddox
D. Jimmy Rollins

Answer on page 31.

13. There are seven players in MLB history to amass 250 home runs, 150 stolen bases, and 100 fielding runs, TWO of them are Phillies—name the duo:
A. Jimmy Rollins & Chase Utley
B. Mike Schmidt & Jimmy Rollins
C. Mike Schmidt & Chase Utley
D. Garry Maddox & Mike Schmidt
Answer on page 32.

14. Which Phillies player had their first big-league hit—a triple—on to Tal's Hill at what was then known as Enron Field?
A. Jimmy Rollins
B. Marlon Anderson
C. Pat Burrell
D. Doug Glanville
Answer on page 32.

15. Which of these Phillies outfielders batted over .400 in 1894?
A. Billy Hamilton
B. Ed Delahanty
C. Sam Thompson
D. Tuck Turner
Answer on page 32.

16. This Phillies player has the most seasons in MLB history with double-digit home runs while reaching at least 20 stolen bases and 30 doubles:
A. Del Enis
B. Jimmy Rollins
C. Chase Utley
D. Bobby Abreu
Answer on page 32.

17. This retired Phillies ballplayer actually has an "active" 293-game errorless streak:
A. Pat Burrell
B. Doug Glanville
C. Jayson Werth
D. Kevin Sefcik
Answer on page 32.

18. Jimmy Rollins set the franchise mark with a hit in 38 straight ballgames in 2006, with 36 of those games coming in 2005, but whose record did he beat?
A. Pete Rose
B. Chuck Klein
C. Willie Montañez
D. Ed Delahanty
Answer on page 32.

19. Which Phillies catcher became the first player in MLB history to hit three home runs in game while calling a shutout as the team's backstop?
A. Benito Santiago
B. Bob Boone
C. Tim McCarver
D. Del Wilber
Answer on page 32.

20. Who holds the Phillies all-time record for most consecutive games reaching base safely?
A. Mike Schmidt
B. Kyle Schwarber
C. Bobby Abreu
D. Odúbel Herrera
Answer on page 32.

21. Let's go for two—how about the Phillies record for most games with at least two times safely on base?
A. Mike Schmidt
B. Pete Rose
C. Richie Ashburn
D. Gavy Cravath
Answer on page 33.

22. Which Phillies player holds the franchise record for most games in a season reaching base safely at least once?
A. Pete Rose
B. Lenny Dykstra
C. Richie Ashburn
D. Bobby Abreu
Answer on page 33.

23. How about most games in a season with at least one hit?
A. Bobby Abreu
B. Pete Rose
C. Chuck Klein
D. Dave Cash
Answer on page 33.

24. Who holds the Phillies single-season record for hits?
A. Chuck Klein
B. Lefty O'Doul
C. Ed Delahanty
D. Richie Ashburn
Answer on page 33.

25. Who was the last Phillies pitcher to both win and save double-digit games in a season?
A. Mitch Williams
B. Gene Garber
C. Jack Baldschun
D. Turk Farrell
Answer on page 33.

26. This Phillies backstop was the inspiration behind *The Natural*:
A. Andy Seminick
B. Gavy Cravath
C. Del Wilber
D. Eddie Waitkus
Answer on page 33.

27. Who was the last Phillies pitcher to hurl three consecutive complete-game shutouts?
A. Cliff Lee
B. Cole Hamels
C. Robin Roberts
D. Grover "Cleveland" Alexander
Answer on page 33.

28. Which batter has the highest all-time batting average at Citizens Bank Ballpark (minimum 200 games played)?
A. Plácido Polanco
B. Trea Turner
C. Bobby Abreu
D. Bryce Harper
Answer on page 34.

29. During the statcast era (since 2015), who has the hardest hit ball for the Phillies in terms of exit velocity?

A. Bryce Harper
B. Kyle Schwarber
C. Jorge Alfaro
D. Aaron Altherr

Answer on page 34.

30. Which Philadelphia team drafted star running back Ricky Williams?

A. Phillies
B. Eagles
C. Sixers
D. Flyers

Answer on page 34.

31. The Phillies once drafted this former Eagles wide receiver:

A. Freddie Mitchell
B. Riley Cooper
C. Chris T. Jones
D. Erving Fryer

Answer on page 34.

32. Who did the Phillies trade for Von Hayes?

A. Jay Baller
B. Julio Franco
C. Manny Trillo
D. George Vukovich

Answer on page 34.

33. This former Phillies player was better known for his accomplishments with another team—and also was a U.S. Army Veteran, an NCAA College Basketball Hall MVP and Hall of Famer, and somehow had more career triples than Rickey Henderson:

A. Tito Francona
B. Dick Groat
C. Cookie Rojas
D. Don Money

Answer on page 34.

34. Who holds the Phillies record for most appearances in a season without losing a game?

A. J. C. Romero
B. Rhéal Cormier
C. Carlos Silva
D. Brad Lidge

Answer on page 34.

35. Who holds the Phillies record for most innings pitched in a season without losing a game?

A. J. C. Romero
B. Rhéal Cormier
C. Carlos Silva
D. Brad Lidge

Answer on page 34.

36. Which former Phillies player called Phillies fans trash, 18 years after he last played there?

A. Ron Gant
B. Alex Arias
C. Desi Relaford
D. Kevin Jordan

Answer on page 34.

37. Who was the first ever Phillies first baseman to have consecutive 100-plus RBI seasons?
A. Don Hurst
B. Rico Brogna
C. Jim Thome
D. Ryan Howard
Answer on page 34.

38. Which position on the diamond, outside of the pitcher, is still without a 100 RBI season in Phillies history?
A. Catcher
B. Shortstop
C. Center fielder
D. Right fielder
Answer on page 35.

39. Which Phillies pitcher has the most starts in franchise history in which he allowed no more than two earned runs but did NOT win the ballgame?
A. Cole Hamels
B. Steve Carlton
D. Robin Roberts
D. Jim Bunning
Answer on page 35.

40. Which Phillies player holds the franchise record for most times safely on base in a season?
A. Billy Hamilton
B. Lefty O'Doul
C. Lenny Dykstra
D. Pete Rose
Answer on page 35.

41. Which Phillies player holds the franchise record for most total bases in a single season?

A. Chuck Klein
B. Dick Allen
C. Ryan Howard
D. Jimmy Rollins

Answer on page 35.

42. Who was the last Phillies player to have more extra-base hits than strikeouts in a qualified season?

A. Jimmy Rollins
B. Plácido Polanco
C. Gregg Jefferies
D. Lenny Dykstra

Answer on page 35.

43. Who holds the Phillies record for most games caught in a season?

A. Bob Boone
B. Darren Daulton
C. Bo Díaz
D. Mike Lieberthal

Answer on page 35.

44. Only one player ever has homered, stolen a base, and also pitched in a game for the Phillies—who was it?

A. Cliff Lee
B. Roman Quinn
C. Jeff Francoeur
D. Robert Person

Answer on page 35.

45. Which Phillies player hit both a game-tying home run and a go-ahead home run in extra innings of a game that he did not even start?

A. Steve Jeltz
B. Raúl Ibañez
C. Matt Stairs
D. John Mayberry Jr.

Answer on page 35.

46. Which offensive stat category does Bobby Abreu lead Tony Gwynn in?

A. On-base percentage
B. Times safely on base
C. Runs scored
D. Extra-base hits

Answer on page 36.

47. Where should Bryce Harper bat to optimize the Phillies offense?

A. Leadoff
B. Second
C. Third
D. Fourth

Answer on page 36.

48. This Phillies player had four straight seasons with at least 30 doubles, 10 triples, 15 home runs, and 30 stolen bases; no other player in history has had more than two TOTAL:

A. Jimmy Rollins
B. Bobby Abreu
C. Von Hayes
D. Juan Samuel

Answer on page 36.

49. The Phillies moved out of the hitter-friendly confines of the Baker Bowl, which measured just 280 feet to right field and 300 to the rightfield power gap, in June of 1938. Which Phillie has led the franchise in batting average AT HOME since (minimum 500 plate appearances)?
A. Richie Ashburn
B. Tony González
C. John Kruk
D. Jim Eisenreich
Answer on page 36.

50. Mike Schmidt's final career hit was a:
A. Single
B. Double
C. Triple
D. Home run
Answer on page 36.

51. Who was the last Phillies player-manager?
A. Jim Fregosi
B. Ben Chapman
C. Bucky Harris
D. Stuff McInnis
Answer on page 36.

52. If the Phillies were to win 100 games, assuming a 162-game season, each season, in what year would they finally cross back over the .500 mark as a franchise?
A. 2032
B. 2044
C. 2054
D. 2086
Answer on page 36.

53. Bobby Abreu actually had a higher career on-base percentage than Ichiro, but how much higher—what is the maximum number of strikeouts that Bobby Abreu could have in a row and still have a higher on-base average than Ichiro if he were to return to baseball?

A. 78
B. 476
C. 617
D. 1,139

Answer on page 36.

54. Seven players in MLB history have totaled at least 300 home runs and 175 fielding runs. They are Barry Bonds, Cal Ripken Jr., Carl Yastrzemski, Willie Mays, Adrian Beltré, Andruw Jones, and which player to don Phillies pinstripes?

A. Mike Schmidt
B. Chase Utley
C. Scott Rolen
D. Ryne Sandberg

Answer on page 37.

55. Who is the only Phillies player to lead the league in hits with at least as many stolen bases as he had strikeout since Ed Delahanty did it in 1899?

A. Richie Ashburn
B. Larry Bowa
C. Jimmy Rollins
D. Ben Revere

Answer on page 37.

56. Who holds the Phillies single-season record for most multi-home games?
A. Mike Schmidt
B. Jim Thome
C. Ryan Howard
D. Kyle Schwarber
Answer on page 37.

57. Who has the Phillies record for most multi-hit games?
A. Richie Ashburn
B. Jimmy Rollins
C. Mike Schmidt
D. Larry Bowa
Answer on page 37.

58. The Reds lost three straight 1-0 ballgames from April 1–3 in 2025, becoming the first team to do so since the Phillies of what year?
A. 2015
B. 1992
C. 1961
D. 1960
Answer on page 37.

59. Three players in history have hit for the cycle in a game during which they played in both the infield and the outfield. Two of them are Michael Cuddyer and Mike Hegan, the other one is this Phillies player:
A. Weston Wilson
B. Gregg Jefferies
C. Johnny Callison
D. Lave Cross
Answer on page 37.

60. Ryan Howard broke Mike Schimidt's single-season team record of 48 home runs (1980) with 58 of his own in 2006, but whose record did Mike Schmidt take down?
A. Chuck Klein
B. Dick Allen
C. Cy Williams
D. None of the Above
Answer on page 37.

61. Who was the Phillies first ever 30-30 man?
A. Mike Schmidt
B. Juan Samuel
C. Bobby Abreu
D. Jimmy Rollins
Answer on page 37.

62. Who was the first ever Phil to hit 40 home runs in a season?
A. Cy Williams
B. Chuck Klein
C. Dick Allen
D. Mike Schmidt
Answer on page 37.

63. Billy Hamilton won a batting title and led the league in walks for the Phillies in 1891. Since, only one Phillies player has accomplished this feat—who?
A. Billy Hamilton, again
B. Chuck Klein
C. Lefty O'Doul
D. Richie Ashburn
Answer on page 37.

64. Who had the first base hit in Phillies history?
A. Charlie Kelly
B. Jack Clements
C. Deacon McGuire
D. William Purcell
Answer on page 37.

65. Who won the first ever game for the Phillies?
A. John Coleman
B. Art Hagan
C. William Purcell
D. Jack Neagle
Answer on page 37.

66. Who was the Phillies last 30-game winner?
A. Steve Carlton
B. Robin Roberts
C. Grover "Cleveland" Alexander
D. William "Kid" Gleason
Answer on page 38.

67. Who was the last Phillies player to "steal for the cycle" (stealing second, third, and home in the same inning)?
A. Jayson Werth
B. Doug Glanville
C. Pete Rose
D. Sherry Magee
Answer on page 38.

68. Who was the first player to hit 100 home runs in a Phillies uniform?
A. Sam Thompson
B. Ed Delahanty
C. Gavy Cravath
D. Cy Williams
Answer on page 38.

69. Who was the first player to hit 250 home runs in a Phillies uniform?
A. Johnny Callison
B. Chuck Klein
C. Cy Williams
D. Del Ennis
Answer on page 38.

70. Home run no. what made Mike Schmidt the Phillies all-time home run leader?
A. 260
B. 261
C. 382
D. 383
Answer on page 38.

71. Who hold the Phillies single-season record in RBIs?
A. Sam Thompson
B. Chuck Klein
C. Ryan Howard
D. Don Hurst
Answer on page 38.

72. Jimmy Rollins stole 453 bags in a Phillies uniform—how many of them were steals of third?

A. 13

B. 88

C. 98

D. 101

Answer on page 39.

73. Who was the last Phillies player with an extra-base bunt hit?

A. Juan Pierre

B. Odúbel Herrera

C. Ben Revere

D. Bryce Harper

Answer on page 39.

74. How many players in MLB history have a higher single-team tenure (e.g., Reggie Jackson has a tenure with the Yankees, Athletics, Angels, and Orioles) OPS than Bryce Harper has with the Phillies (minimum 125 plate appearances)?

A. 3

B. 5

C. 11

D. None of the Above

Answer on page 39.

75. Bryce Harper during his career, including his time with the Nationals, has 17 home runs with a .390 OBP and a .596 slugging percentage during postseason play—how many players in MLB history best him in all three categories?
A. 3
B. 4
C. 5
D. None of the Above
Answer on page 39.

76. A tribute to '76—in terms of OPS, which Phillies player has had the greatest 76-game stretch in franchise history?
A. Dolph Camili
B. Chuck Klein
C. Ryan Howard
D. Bryce Harper
Answer on page 39

77. Who is the Phillies all-time leader for postseason home runs?
A. Kyle Schwarber
B. Bryce Harper
C. Jayson Werth
D. Chase Utley
Answer on page 39.

78. Who is the Phillies' all-time leader in postseason hits?
A. Jimmy Rollins
B. Shane Victorino
C. Chase Utley
D. Bryce Harper
Answer on page 39.

79. Which former Phillie became the first player ever to hit a grand slam for two different teams during postseason play?
A. Pete Rose
B. Jim Thome
C. Shane Victorino
D. Jayson Werth
Answer on page 39.

80. Chase Utley batted .301/.388/.535 during his five-year peak from 2005 to 2009. Since Jackie Robinson broke the color barrier in 1947, how many other second basemen have batted at least that during any two-year span?
A. 2
B. 3
C. 4
D. 5
Answer on page 40.

81. Harry Kalas dubbed Chase Utley as "The Man," when he did what?
A. Inside-the-park home run
B. Straight steal of home
C. Scored from second on an infield chopper
D. Scored from second on a sacrifice fly
Answer on page 40.

82. When Jimmy Rollins hit 20 triples in 2007, during his 20/20/20/20 campaign, he became the first Phillies player with 20 triples since who?
A. Juan Samuel
B. Johnny Callison
C. Chuck Klein
D. Nap Lajoie
Answer on page 40.

83. Who was the first Phillies player with 30 doubles, 10 triples, and 20 home runs in a season?
A. Jimmy Rollins
B. Bobby Abreu
C. Juan Samuel
D. Cy Williams
Answer on page 40.

84. Which Phillies' pitcher had the greatest season in terms of winning percentage (minimum 20 decisions)?
A. Roy Halladay
B. John Denny
C. Tommy Greene
D. Robin Roberts
Answer on page 40.

85. Which Phillies' catcher is tied with Jason Varitek for the most no-hitters ever caught, with four?
A. Andy Seminick
B. Bob Boone
C. Darren Daulton
D. Carlos Ruiz
Answer on page 40.

86. Who has the Phillies' franchise record for most career grand slams?
A. Mike Schmidt
B. Ryan Howard
C. Pat Burrell
D. Bryce Harper
Answer on page 40.

87. Jimmy Rollins holds the franchise record with 46 lead-off home runs. Whose record did he break?
A. Bake McBride
B. Juan Samuel
C. Lenny Dykstra
D. Doug Glanville
Answer on page 40.

88. The Phillies single-season home-run record was set by who and when?
A. Jimmy Rollins, 2007
B. Jimmy Rollins, 2012
C. Kyle Schwarber, 2023
D. Kyle Schwarber, 2024
Answer on page 40.

89. Who holds the Phillies all-time record for pinch hits?
A. Greg Gross
B. Tony Taylor
C. Rubén Amaro Jr.
D. Greg Dobbs
Answer on page 40.

90. Who was the last Phillies pitcher with a shutout intact through 10 innings?
A. Roy Halladay
B. Cliff Lee
C. Curt Schilling
D. Steve Carlton
Answer on page 40.

91. This Phillies pitcher remains the last pitcher to hurl a complete-game shutout with his team facing World Series elimination:

A. Curt Schilling
B. Cole Hamels
C. Cliff Lee
D. Zack Wheeler

Answer on page 41.

92. Who was the last Phillie to score from second base on a sacrifice fly?

A. Brian R. Hunter
B. Brian L. Hunter
C. Johan Rojas
D. Doug Glanville

Answer on page 41.

93. Who was the last Phillie to have multiple bunt base hits in a game?

A. Otto Kemp
B. Garrett Stubbs
C. Bryce Harper
D. Johan Rojas

Answer on page 41.

94. Philadelphia's 94.1 WIP Host Jack Fritz is said to have saved the career (and possibly the life) of which Phillie ballplayer?

A. Jonathan Papelbon
B. Nick Pivetta
C. Mickey Moniak
D. Trea Turner

Answer on page 41

95. Who was the last Phillie to have multiple triples in a game?
A. Odúbel Herrera
B. Nick Williams
C. Freddy Galvis
D. Shane Victorino
Answer on page 41.

96. Who was the last Phillie to "out hit" the cycle (meaning at least four hits, including a double, triple, and a home run, but no single)?
A. Bryce Harper
B. Kyle Schwarber
C. Ryan Howard
D. John Kruk
Answer on page 41.

97. Which player hit a walk-off grand slam with the Phillies down three runs and down to their final out?
A. Brad Miller
B. Bo Díaz
C. Bryce Harper
D. John Kruk
Answer on page 42.

98. Who was the last Phillie to hit a walk-off single with the team trailing and down to their last strike?
A. Bryson Stott
B. Pat Burrell
C. Garrett Stubbs
D. Travis Lee
Answer on page 42.

99. Which former Phillies player admitted to hiring a private investigator to dig up dirt on umpires so that he could hold it over their heads in hopes of getting a more favorable strike zone?

A. Lenny Dykstra
B. Ugueth Urbina
C. Ricky Jordan
D. Steve Jeltz

Answer on page 42.

100. The Phillies sent two representatives as All-Stars in the 1999 All-Star Game at Fenway Park, who were they?

A. Curt Schilling & Scott Rolen
B. Curt Schilling & Doug Glanville
C. Scott Rolen & Bobby Abreu
D. Curt Schilling & Paul Byrd

Answer on page 42.

GOIN' DEEP: 100 QUESTIONS & INCREDIBLE STORIES

ANSWERS

1. C—Cody Asche. Cody Asche is the only Phillies player—and the most recent major leaguer—to hit a walk-off home run on the same date in consecutive seasons, doing so on September 12, 2014, with a two-run shot in the bottom of the 10th off the Marlins' Dan Jennings, then repeating the feat on September 12, 2015, with another two-run homer in the bottom of the ninth off the Cubs' Héctor Rondón. He joins Nick Swisher, Adrian Beltre, Cory Snyder, Jack Clark, Duffy Dyer, Jimmie Hall, and Don Lock as the only players in history to accomplish this feat.

2. B—Tommy Joseph. It might surprise fans expecting names like Mike Schmidt, Ryan Howard, or Pat Burrell, but Tommy Joseph stands alone as the only player in franchise history to hit at least 20 home runs in each of his first two big-league seasons—which were also his only big-league seasons—with 21 in 2016 and 22 in 2017. Burrell and Hoskins each hit 18 in their debut seasons, Don Hurst had 19-plus in his first two, and Howard's "first" season was a brief 2004 cameo with just two homers.

3. A—Cameron Rupp. J. T. Realmuto joined the short list on July 3, 2022, by becoming the first Phillies catcher to hit a home run, steal a base, and gun down a runner, but it was Cameron Rupp who did it first on June 16, 2017, marking the franchise's initial such triple-feat since caught stealing was officially tracked in 1951. All four backstops, along with Jorge Alfaro, had games with a home run and a stolen base, but Rupp and Realmuto stand alone with the gunned-down runner.

4. B—Pat Burrell. The fleet-footed Pat Burrell was well known for stealing during his tenure in Philadelphia, just not bases . . . his great on-base prowess let him reach base often and stay there safely. He went 1,244 games straight without being caught stealing from August 15, 2001, to June 27, 2010, outdone only by Paul Konerko (1,360) since caught stealing became an official statistic in 1951.

5. D—Cole Hamels. Cole Hamels no-hit the Cubs on July 25, 2015, handing Jake Arrieta his sole defeat in a 31-start span where Arrieta posted a 1.09 ERA and threw two no-hitters himself, proving that the only way to beat him during that dominant run was to literally beat him at his own game . . . with a no-hitter.

6. A—Ed Delahanty. On August 28, 2025, Kyle Schwarber crushed four home runs against the Braves, making the Phillies the only franchise in MLB history with four different players to accomplish the feat—joining Mike Schmidt (1976), Chuck Klein (1936), and the original four-homer king, "Big Ed" Delahanty (1896). It was Delahanty, however, whose story ended in one of baseball's darkest chapters: in 1903, deep in a bender after abandoning the Washington Senators, the drunken Hall of Famer was kicked off a train and onto the International Railway Bridge at 2 a.m., then fell—or was pushed—into the raging Niagara River on July 2. Two weeks later his battered body washed up twenty miles downstream, naked except for his tie, socks, and shoes—proving, perhaps for the first time in history, that shit really does happen when you party naked.

7. D—Jim Eisenreich. Known for his ticks, on the field and in the hit column, at .324, Jimmy Eisenreich leads the way. Abreu hit .303, Kruk .309, and Klein played to majority of hit Hall of Fame career in the Baker Bowl.

8. A—Kyle Schwarber. Schwarber leads the way at just 15.00 plate-appearances-per-home-runs after his 56-homer season in 2024. Thome is second at 16.13, followed by Howard at 17.10, then Schmidt at 18.36—unless you set the minimum to 50 homers, then Schmidt is edged out by Pete Incaviglia at 18.25.

9. B—Cliff Lee. Lee had 207 strikeouts to just 28 bases on balls in 2012, the first pitcher to reach 200 strikeouts in a season without walking 30 batters. Halladay came close in 2010, when he struck out 219, but walked 30 on the nose. Nola actually accomplished this feat later, in 2022, and Schilling had a season with Arizona where he walked all of 33 batters with 316 (!) strikeouts in 2002.

10. A—Aaron Nola. Nola accomplished this feat on June 25, 2021, a game in which Nola also tied Tom Seaver for the most consecutive strikeouts in a game, with 10.

11. D—Three or more. Not one, not two, not three . . . or four, or five, or six, but SEVEN three-ball counts during his perfect game, including three of the first four batters he faced. Nearly imperfect, to us, makes it even more perfect—the epitome of the gamer who was Roy Halladay.

12. D—Jimmy Rollins. Grandy-Man can and so could J-Roll. In 2007, Jimmy Rollins became not just one of four 20/20/20/20 players in MLB history, but the ONLY ever to total 20 triples,

30 home runs, and 40 stolen bases in a season (in fact, you can make that just 20 home runs, and it still holds true).

13. C—Mike Schmidt and Chase Utley. Schmidt and Utley are on a list of baseball royalty, alongside Barry Bonds, Willie Mays, Carl Yastrzemski, Andruw Jones, and Mookie Betts.

14. C—Pat Burrell. One of these men is not like the others, one of these men—it's always the one you least expect . . . or is it?

15. Trick question! They ALL batted north of .400, with Hamilton at .403, Big Ed at .405, Sam Thompson at .415, and Tuck Turner leading the way as a fourth outfielder batting .418 in "limited time" with 382 plate appearances.

16. D—Bobby Abreu. In fact, it is not even close—Bobby has 11 total, including SEVEN with the Phillies; those seven alone equal Barry Bonds's career total . . . and Bonds ranks second all-time.

17. B—Doug Glanville.

18. D—Ed Delahanty. There's that name again! Big Ed had a 31-gamer in 1899.

19. D—Del Wilber. Wilber played one of the finest games in MLB history, on August 27, 1951, catching the second leg of a doubleheader, hitting a solo home run in each of his three times at the plate, single-handed leading (and calling) the Phils to a 3–0 victory over the Reds. Wilber has since been joined by Don Leppert on April 11, 1963, and Ivan Rodriguez on September 11, 1997.

20. A—Mike Schmidt. This time it wasn't the odd man out—Mike Schmidt reached in 56 straight from August 16, 1981, to May 8, 1982. It might seem strange seeing Odúbel in there, but he did have 44 straight from September 27, 2017, to May 19, 2018. Only Klein (49), Schwarber (47), and Abreu (48) have had longer streaks.

21. B—Pete Rose. Charlie Hustle, at the ripe age of thirty-eight, had 20 straight games reaching base safely twice—a stretch that saw him bat .500/.589/.603 with 39 base hits, 16 walks, and one hit-by-pitch. That year he played in 163 games, reaching twice in 100 of them!

22. D—Bobby Abreu.

23. C—Chuck Klein. Chuk Klein hit safely in 135 games in 1930, en route to a .386/436/.687 season with 250 hits—surely a Phillies single-season record, right . . . ?

24. B—Lefty O'Doul. O'Doul smashed 254 hits in 1929, but it wasn't enough, as he fell just one hit shy of .400, batting .398 on the season . . . but he did reach on error seven times that year; think it is too late for a scorebook review?

25. A—Mitch Williams. Turns out, all four of them did it, but Mitch was the last to do so in 1991; add in Jim Konstanty in 1950, and you've got every pitcher in team history to accomplish the feat—with Farrell and Baldschun each doing it twice!

26. D—Eddie Waitkus. Waitkus was one of the most decorated ballplayers of World War II, earning TEN meritorious service awards in the United States Army, including four Bronze Stars. More adept at evading fire from enemies than his own fans, he was shot by a young, obsessed female stalker when the Phillies were visiting Chicago on June 14, 1949.

27. A—Cliff Lee. Lee had three straight in June of 2011; had the question said four, the answer would have been Mr. President!

28. A—Plácido Polanco. They rank 1–4, respectively, at .310, .304, .302, and .296—if you only count their time with the home team, Harper and Abreu swap spots and their averages are then .311, .307, .299, and .299.

29. B—Kyle Schwarber. All of them appear near the top, but Kyle Schwarber takes it with his 117.2 mph double off former teammate Michael Lorenzen on September 12, 2025.

30. A—Phillies. Okay, this one was a gimme, but I bet you didn't know that the Phillies had taken Ricky Williams long before the Dirty-30 wanted the Eagles to draft him—but they did, in the eighth round and 213th overall in the 1995 draft as a shortstop out of Patrick Henry High School.

31. B—Riley Cooper. I know you were thinking FredEx, but he was taken by the Rays in 1997 and the White Sox in 2000, after sharing a ballfield with Chase Utley at UCLA. The Phillies took Riley Cooper 457th overall in 2006.

32. His nickname was Five-for-One not Four-for-One; they gave up all four of them in addition to Jerry Willard.

33. B—Dick Groat. A life well lived. Hall of Fame in our book!

34. D–Brad Lidge. All four had seasons in which they didn't take a loss for the Phils, but Lidge did so with the most appearances, at 72, during his perfect 2008 season—our perfect season.

35. B—Rhéal Cormier. Similar question, same choices, but different result—84.2 innings from Rhéal Cormier in 2003.

36. C—Desi Relaford. Alright, dude . . . why don't you hop on your baseball-reference page and tell me why . . .

37. B—Rico Brogna. Brogna was the first when he did it in 1998 and 1999.

38. B—Shortstop. Catcher has had two both by Darren Daulton, in 1992 and 1993, center field has seen just one with Cy Williams in 1923, and right field has more than any other position with 26. Shortstop stands alone.

39. A—Cole Hamels. Hamels leads the way with 86 starts in which he allowed no more than two earned runs but did not win the ballgame—he was 0-30 with a 1.84 ERA, averaging 20 outs per start in those.

40. A—Billy Hamilton. How about 362 times safely on base in just 132 games played!

41. A—Chuck Klein. Good for 445 total bases during his incredible season in 1930, but then again . . . see the dimensions of The Baker Bowl—and we are still holding Coors Field against potential Hall of Famers?

42. A—Jimmy Rollins. All four of them did it, Rollins (2), Polanco (1), Jefferies (3), and Dykstra (1), but Rollins was the most recent.

43. B—Darren Daulton. Okay, technically this one is a tie, Dutch and Boonie both had season with 146 games caught, in 1993 and 1974, respectively, but Daulton caught 43 more innings, so I've got to give him the edge. Partial credit if you answered Boone!

44. B—Roman Quinn. On August 2, 2019, Roman Quinn hurled two strong innings in relief; unfortunately, that, plus his speed and pop was not enough, as the Phillies fell to the White Sox, 4–3, in 15 innings.

45. D—John Mayberry Jr. On June 4, 2013, Mayberry Jr. pinch-hit and struck out in the bottom of the seventh before hitting a game-tying home run in the bottom of the 10th and following it up with a walk-off grand slam in the 11th.

46. That is right, and not just that—slugging, OPS, home runs, RBI, and stolen bases, all Bobby. There is one category that he doesn't lead Mr. Padre in, and while hits is true, that is not what I am thinking . . . plate appearances. Abreu reached base safely 24 more times than Tony Gwynn did in his career, despite 151 fewer plate appearances.

47. A—Leadoff. Statistically, the leadoff spot will have the greatest number of opportunities to have a direct impact on the game's outcome, and that is not just because they are coming up in a 0-0 ballgame at least 81 times per year, as it holds true throughout the game, becoming even more evident in fact. This is not an opinion; this is just the reality of the situation.

48. D—Juan Samuel. Samuel did this every season from 1984 through 1987, becoming the first player with two straight since Jimmy Ryan in 1888 and 1889. No one has had consecutive such seasons since, and no one else has more than two total.

49. D—Jim Eisenreich

50. A—Single. That may seem boring, but it, in fact, is not—as it was a bunt single, on May 25, 1989.

51. B—Ben Chapman. Chapman was the Phillies last player-manager, in 1945 and 1946. In his limited role as a player, just 25 games, he batted .308.

52. C—2054. 162–0 going forward gets us there in 2032, 110–52 in 2044, 100–62 in 2054, and 90–2 in 2086 . . .

53. D—1,139. Seven players in MLB history have totaled at least 300 home runs and 175 fielding runs, they are Barry Bonds, Cal Ripken Jr., Carl Yastrzemski, Willie Mays, Adrian Beltré, Andruw Jones, and which player to don Phillies pinstripes:

54. C—Scott Rolen.

55. D—Ben Revere.

56. D—Kyle Schwarber. Schwarber hit eight in 2022, a record he cannot even seem to touch, with three in 2023, six in 2024, and five in 2025.

57. B—Jimmy Rollins. It should come as no surprise that J-Roll leads here, but what may be a surprise is by how much—just ONE more than Richie Ashburn!

58. D—1960.

59. A—Weston Wilson. All four of these Phillies hit for the cycle, but only Weston Wilson did so playing in the infield and the outfield, on August 15, 2024.

60. D—None of the Above. In 1980, when Mike Schmidt hit 48 home runs, he actually toppled his own record, of 45, set the year prior, but when he did it in 1979, he bested the 1929 record of 43, by Chuck Klein.

61. C—Bobby Abreu. Bobby Abreu became the Phillies first 30-30 man in 2001, and then repeated the feat in 2004. He was since joined by Jimmy Rollins in 2007. Mike Schmidt fell just one stolen base shy of the club in 1975.

62. A—Cy Williams. Williams had 41 home runs in 1923.

63. D—Richie Ashburn.

64. D—William Purcell. Left fielder William "Blondie" Purcell got the Phillies' first hit and scored the first run on May 1, 1883.

65. D—Jack Neagle. Neagle won the Phillies first game on May 14, 1883—bringing the franchise record to 1–8—against the Chicago White Stockings. It was his only ever win for the Phils.

Our Phils have played a total of 21,810 games as a franchise, and in all but one of them—the first—they have been a lifetime sub-.500 ballclub.

66. C—Grover Cleveland Alexander. Three times Alexander won 30 games for the Phillies, in 1915, 1916, and 1917. Carlton probably would have gotten there in 1972, with 27 of their 59 total victories—he was 11–0 in 12 games in which he allowed no earned runs, and he was 16–10 with a 2.88 ERA in the 21 games when he did allow an earned run.

67. A—Jayson Werth. Werth accomplished this on May 12, 2009, against the Dodgers. The only other Phillies to do this are listed, Pete Rose (May 11, 1980) and Sherry Magee (July 12, 1906)—with apologies to Doug Glanville.

68. C—Gavy Cravath. Cravath hit a two-run, game-tying home run in the bottom of the ninth inning off Pirates' Bob Steele on June 17, 1918, it was the 101st home run of his career but his 100th in a Phillies' uniform.

69. D—Del Ennis. Del Ennis hit the 250th home run of his career, all with the Phillies, in the second game of a double-header on July 22, 1956, a solo shot off Milwaukee Braves' Lew Burdette in the fifth inning.

70. A—260. Mike Schmidt hit home run No. 260 in the first inning on July 26, 1980, in the first game of a doubleheader on July 25, 1980, giving him the franchise all-time lead over Del Ennis. That wasn't enough for Michael Jack, so he hit No. 261 his very next time up—then a few more . . .

71. B—Chuck Klein. Chuck Klein had a franchise record 170 RBIs in 1930; incredibly, he was 21 off the league leader, Hack Wilson, who had a major-league record 191 that season.

72. C—98. Don't worry—Jimmy got his 100th with the Dodgers, and then 101 with the White Sox.

73. B—Odúbel Herrera. Herrera laid down a hard bunt down the third baseline with the bases loaded against the Rockies on September 11, 2021, knocking in two and going for two bases.

74. A—3. The only players who bested Bryce's 1.090 OPS in the postseason as a Phil are Babe Ruth with the Yankees, Lou Gehrig with the Yankees, and Barry Bonds with the Giants. For the record, Reggie also had a 1.090 OPS with the Yankees, but his is rounded up to 1.090, Harper's is rounded down to it.

75. D—None of the Above. The answer is none of the above, because it is no none—no player in history has as many home runs and as high of an on-base percentage and slugging percentage as Bryce Harper has during postseason play in his career.

76. C—Ryan Howard. Ryan Howard put together a 76-game stretch from July 14, 2006, to April 2, 2007, during which he batted .357/.510/.747—a 1.257 OPS! Bashing 30 home runs with 78 RBIs. Don't like that it spanned two seasons, then look to his final 76 games of 2006, when he posted a 1.243 OPS with the same 30 home runs and 78 RBI. Prime Big Piece was a FORCE!

77. A—Kyle Schwarber. 14 Schwarbombs and counting . . .

78. A—Jimmy Rollins & B—Shane Victorino. Both are correct—they are tied for the lead at 47 apiece.

79. C—Shane Victorino. Victorino became the second player ever with multiple career postseason grand slams when he hit his second with the Red Sox in 2013. Jim Thome was the first with a pair, but both with the Indians. Francisco Lindor has since joined both groups, but let's not talk about that . . .

80. B—3. Joe Morgan from 1975–76, Jeff Kent from 1999–2000 and 2000–01, and Jose Altuve from 2016–17. You will note that EVERY stretch there includes at least one MVP Award.

81. C—Scored from second on an infield chopper. Utley scored from second on Ryan Howard's infield chopper to Braves' pitcher Macay McBride following his own bases loaded, bases clearing, go-ahead double in the top of the seventh inning, on August 9, 2006.

82. D—Nap Lajoie. J-Roll was the first with 20 triples since Nap Lajoie did it way back in 1897.

83. D—Cy Williams. Cy Williams became the first back in 1924, with 31 doubles, 11 triples, and 24 home runs.

84. Both C and D—Greene went 16–4 in 1993, and Roberts was 28–7 in 1952—both good for an .800 winning percentage.

85. D—Carlos Ruiz. Ruiz caught four of the 14 no-hitters; no other catcher has more than one in franchise history.

86. B—Ryan Howard. Howard leads the way with 15, more than double Mike Schmidt's career total of seven.

87. B—Juan Samuel. Samuel had 14. In a twist, Kyle Schwarber would also break this record . . . in 2024, alone, with 15 (33, total).

88. D—Kyle Schwarber, 2024. Schwarber hit not just a Phillies' record, but a major-league record 15 leadoff home runs in 2024.

89. A—Greg Gross. Gross had 117 total pinch hits for the Phillies, more than double the second place Tony Taylor at 54.

90. B—Cliff Lee. Cliff Lee went 10 shutout innings on just 102 pitches against the Giants on April 18, 2012, his effort resulted in a no-decision and a Phillies loss . . . it was then I knew, the run was over.

91. A—Curt Schilling. Schilling tossed a complete-game shutout over the Blue Jays in Game Five of the World Series with the Phils down, 3–1 in the series, on October 21, 1993. In his postseason career, he made three starts with his team able to clinch—his team won all three games, and he had a 1.15 ERA—and five starts with his team facing elimination—his team won all five games, and he had a 1.37 ERA. He is the most clutch postseason pitcher in baseball history.

92. B—Brian L. Hunter. Hunter scored from second base on a deep flyball to centerfield hit by Doug Glanville on April 3, 2001. Doug had a propensity to be involved in these plays, as he, himself, scored from second on a ball hit to center by Scott Rolen on July 24, 1998. Both times this happened, it came against the Marlins!

93. B—Garrett Stubbs. Stubbs had a pair of bunt base hits against—you guessed it—the Marlins on September 7, 2024, laying down one each in the top of the third and fifth innings off pitcher Darren McCaughan.

94. D—Trea Turner. Turner batted .337/.389/.668 in the final 48 games of the 2023 season, after the "Captain" Jack Fritz Standing Ovation Intervention.

95. A—Odúbel Herrera. Once again, they've all done it, but Herrera was the last—on August 9, 2017, in a 3–2 victory over the Braves, just three weeks after Nick Williams had his own.

96. C—Ryan Howard. Big Piece went 4-for-4 with a double, triple, and two home runs on June 18, 2010, in a 9–5 win over the Twins—it doesn't go down as a cycle, but to me, these games are far more impressive!

97. B—Bo Díaz. All four players hit walk-off slams for the Phil, but only Bo Diaz hit one with the team trailing by three and down to their final out, doing so to cap off a five-run ninth-inning comeback victory of the Mets on April 13, 1983. His grand slam came off of Neil Allen, who, oddly, is the last pitcher to officially throw a shutout in relief (per MLB Handbook, p. 140, Rule 9.18, lines 2–6, a pitcher can toss a shutout without a complete game should he come in relief and no outs are recorded and no runs have yet scored). This was just one of two instances ever where it occurred—the other came on June 23, 1917, when Ernie Shore went 26-up, 27-down in relief of Babe Ruth, who was ejected after punching the home-plate umpire after walking the first batter. That runner was caught stealing, and Shore retired the next 26 batters consecutively. Originally, this was ruled a perfect game, but it is now correctly considered a combined no-hitter . . . so Babe Ruth is actually credited with starting a combined no-hitter. All of this to say, simply, that it is NOT actually redundant to say complete-game shutout, and it is, in fact, not only correct, but it is the only correct way to phrase it—unless of course it was done by a reliever, but I digress . . .

98. C—Garrett Stubbs. Stubber can bunt for hits, hit clutch walk-off home runs—does it all while Dancing on His Own! He hit a three-run, walk-off home run on June 15, 2022, with the Phillies trailing, 1-0, on a 2-2, two-out pitch off Marlins' Tanner Scott.

99. A—Lenny Dykstra. Dykstra talked about doing exactly this in his autobiography, *House of Nails*. Dude was on his game.

100. D—Curt Schilling and Paul Byrd. If character defined who was or was not an All-Star or even a Hall of Famer, I know for sure Paul Byrd would be there every year and not residing in Cooperstown. As for Schilling—he won every single "character" award MLB had to offer, and the same writers who refused to vote for him for the Hall of Fame gave them to him. I wonder why they changed their minds . . . first ballot from where I stand.

GENERAL ADMISSION

QUESTIONS

From basic to bizarre, these questions cover a lot of ground.

1. Who holds the Phillies' highest career batting average?
   A. Billy Hamilton
   B. Ed Delahanty
   C. Richie Ashburn
   D. Chuck Klein
   Answer on page 71.

2. Who holds the Phillies' highest career slugging percentage?
   A. Dick Allen
   B. Mike Schmidt
   C. Chuck Klein
   D. Kyle Schwarber
   Answer on page 71.

3. Who's scored the most runs in team history?
   A. Jimmy Rollins
   B. Mike Schmidt
   C. Richie Ashburn
   D. Ed Delahanty
   Answer on page 71.

4. Who has the most career triples in team history?
A. Sherry Magee
B. Jimmy Rollins
C. Richie Ashburn
D. Ed Delahanty
Answer on page 71.

5. Who has the highest hit-by-pitch total with the Phillies?—over twice as many as anyone else in team history!
A. Mike Lieberthal
B. Larry Bowa
C. Chase Utley
D. Mike Schmidt
Answer on page 71.

6. Who knocked in the winning run in Game Five of the 2008 World Series?
A. Eric Bruntlett
B. Pedro Feliz
C. Geoff Jenkins
D. Pat Burrell
Answer on page 71.

7. Who is the only Phillies player born in Alaska?
A. Josh Phelps
B. Rhéal Cormier
C. Paul Byrd
D. Curt Schilling
Answer on page 71.

8. Which Canadian-born player has the highest career Phillies WAR, according to Baseball-Reference.com?
A. Nick Pivetta
B. Rhéal Cormier
C. Ferguson Jenkins
D. Randy Wolf
Answer on page 71.

9. Shane "The Flyin' Hawaiian" Victorino holds the record for most All-Star appearances for Hawaii-born MLB players (two). He shares the record with Kirby Yates and this former Phillie:
A. Charlie Hough
B. Jerome Williams
C. J. T. Realmuto
D. Sid Fernandez
Answer on page 71.

10. Only three Nicaraguan players in history have made an MLB All-Star Game. Which one represented the Phillies?
A. Raul Ibañez
B. Porfi Altamirano
C. Odúbel Herrera
D. Vicente Padilla
Answer on page 72.

11. What season did the Phillie Phanatic make his debut?
A. 1972
B. 1974
C. 1976
D. 1978
Answer on page 72.

12. Phanatic costume designer Bonnie Erickson is credited with designing which iconic Muppet?
A. Kermit the Frog
B. Miss Piggy
C. Grover
D. Fozzie Bear
Answer on page 72.

13. The father of Dave Raymond, the first person to portray the Phillie Phanatic, head coached which sport at the University of Maine?
A. Baseball
B. Football
C. Basketball
D. Ping-pong
Answer on page 72.

14. Who was the primary inspiration for the Phillie Phanatic?
A. Mr. Met
B. Brutus Buckeye
C. The San Diego Chicken
D. Youppi!
Answer on page 72.

15. Upset with the Phanatic beating up on a dummy wearing the opposing team's uniform in 1988, which MLB manager said the following: "If he wants to entertain, dance, carry kids around, that's great. But I don't believe in demonstrating violence at the ballpark, and that's what he does with the dummy."
A. Tony LaRussa
B. Jim Leyland
C. Tommy Lasorda
D. Bobby Cox
Answer on page 72.

16. Which publication declared the Phanatic "the best mascot ever" in 2000?

A. *Forbes*

B. *Time*

C. *Sports Illustrated*

D. *Sports Illustrated for Kids*

Answer on page 72.

17. According to the Phillies, where does the Phanatic originally hail from?

A. The Galapagos Islands

B. The Maldives

C. Madagascar

D. Turks and Caicos

Answer on page 72.

18. Which three mascots, as of 2026, are the only mascots on display at the National Baseball Hall of Fame and Museum in Cooperstown?

A. The Phillie Phanatic

B. Mr. Met

C. Bernie Brewer

D. Youppi!

E. The San Diego Chicken

F. Billy the Marlin

G. Blooper

H. Fredbird

I. Mr. Red

J. The Oriole Bird

Answer on page 72.

19. Who holds the single-season record for at-bats per home run?

A. Rhys Hoskins
B. Ryan Howard
C. Kyle Schwarber
D. Mike Schmidt

Answer on page 73.

20. Who holds the career mark for at-bats per home run?

A. Rhys Hoskins
B. Ryan Howard
C. Kyle Schwarber
D. Mike Schmidt

Answer on page 73.

21. The Phillies have been around for a VERY long time. They've had every numerical season win total from 49 to 97, except for one. Which is it?

A. 53
B. 60
C. 70
D. 93

Answer on page 73.

22. How many times have the Phillies played 163 games?

A. Never
B. Once
C. Twice
D. Thrice

Answer on page 73.

23. What's the team record for losses in a single season?

A. 110
B. 111
C. 112
D. 113

Answer on page 73.

24. There have been 15 unassisted triple plays in MLB history. Eric Bruntlett turned the last one for Philadelphia; which Phillie is credited with the first?

A. Larry Bowa
B. Mickey Morandini
C. Manny Trillo
D. Tony Taylor

Answer on page 73.

25. Who was the shortest player in franchise history?

A. Billy Maharg
B. Bobby Shantz
C. Charles Yingling
D. Ricky Otero

Answer on page 73.

26. Who was the tallest?

A. Michael Schwimer
B. Elvis Araújo
C. Aaron Harang
D. Ryan Madson

Answer on page 73.

27. What was the franchise's first single-season home-run record?

A. 1
B. 2
C. 3
D. 4

Answer on page 73.

28. Who is the first Hall of Fame manager to have played for the Phillies?

A. Jim Leyland
B. Tommy Lasorda
C. Casey Stengel
D. Sparky Anderson

Answer on page 73.

29. Who is the only Phillies manager to have two separate stints as skipper with the team?

A. Danny Ozark
B. Gene Mauch
C. Burt Shotton
D. Eddie Sawyer

Answer on page 74.

30. The Phillies have had 12 seasons with a total attendance over three million. Which season did they draw the most fans?

A. 1980
B. 2008
C. 2010
D. 2025

Answer on page 74.

31. Who is the only Phillie to play a 163-game season?

A. Bobby Abreu
B. Larry Bowa
C. Scott Rolen
D. Pete Rose

Answer on page 74.

32. How many no. 1 overall MLB draft picks have donned a Phillies jersey?

A. 10
B. 13
C. 16
D. 19

Answer on page 74.

33. How many no. 1 overall MLB draft picks were drafted by and played for the Phillies?

A. 3
B. 5
C. 7
D. 9

Answer on page 74.

34. Who has the career record for grand slams?

A. Ryan Howard
B. Mike Schmidt
C. Kyle Schwarber
D. Bryce Harper

Answer on page 74.

35. Who has the highest career postseason OPS (on-base + slugging percentage; min. 50 at-bats)?
A. Bryce Harper
B. Chase Utley
C. Gary Matthews
D. Jayson Werth
Answer on page 74.

36. Who has the lowest career postseason ERA mark (minimum 40 IP)?
A. Cliff Lee
B. Cole Hamels
C. Ranger Suarez
D. Zack Wheeler
Answer on page 74.

37. Who's had the most at-bats for the Phillies without an extra-base hit?
A. Joe Blanton
B. Cy Blanton
C. Don Carman
D. Paul Byrd
Answer on page 74.

38. In 1883, John Coleman set the team record for most losses in a single season. How many losses did Coleman have in 61 starts that season?
A. 22
B. 34
C. 48
D. 25
Answer on page 74.

39. There are 10 Phillies who have recorded at least 1,000 strikeouts in red pinstripes; who is not a part of that list?

A. Zack Wheeler
B. Curt Simmons
C. Aaron Nola
D. Brett Myers

Answer on page 74.

40. There have only been five seasons in which a Phillies reliever collected over 40 saves. Only one player has accomplished it twice. Who is he?

A. Billy Wagner
B. Brad Lidge
C. José Mesa
D. Steve Bedrosian
E. Jonathan Papelbon

Answer on page 75.

41. Which Phillies pitcher holds the record for most games played (pitched) in a single season?

A. J. C. Romero
B. Ryan Madson
C. Rhéal Cormier
D. Kent Tekulve
E. Hector Neris

Answer on page 75.

42. Who holds the record for the most complete-game shutouts in a single season?

A. Steve Carlton
B. Cole Hamels
C. Curt Schilling
D. Robin Roberts
E. Grover Cleveland Alexander

Answer on page 75.

43. Which Phillies pitcher allowed 43 home runs during the 2004 season?

A. Vicente Padilla
B. Eric Milton
C. Cory Lidle
D. Brian Powell

Answer on page 75.

44. What year did the Phillies pitching staff record the most strikeouts in a single season?

A. 1997
B. 2021
C. 2008
D. 2012

Answer on page 75.

45. Who holds the team record for most wild pitches with 120?

A. Mitch Williams
B. Chris Short
C. Steve Carlton
D. Ed Daily

Answer on page 75.

46. How many home runs did the 2004 Phillies pitching staff allow?

A. 349
B. 153
C. 214
D. 198

Answer on page 75.

47. Who was the only Phillie to not allow an earned run during the 2008 postseason?

A. Brad Lidge
B. Cole Hamels
C. J. C. Romero
D. Chad Durbin
E. J. A. Happ

Answer on page 75.

48. Who led the team in strikeouts in 2008?

A. Brett Myers
B. Kyle Kendrick
C. Cole Hamels
D. Jamie Moyer

Answer on page 75.

49. Who led the team in saves in 2022?

A. Jose Alvarado
B. Seranthony Dominguez
C. Corey Knebel
D. David Robertson

Answer on page 75.

50. Who led the team in innings pitched in 2009?
A. Joe Blanton
B. Jamie Moyer
C. Cole Hamels
D. Cliff Lee
E. J. A. Happ
Answer on page 75.

51. Who led the team in strikeouts during the 2009 postseason?
A. Pedro Martinez
B. Joe Blanton
C. Cliff Lee
D. Cole Hamels
Answer on page 75.

52. Who lead the 1993 Phillies in strikeouts?
A. Ben Rivera
B. Terry Mulholland
C. Danny Jackson
D. Curt Schilling
E. Tommy Greene
Answer on page 76.

53. Which Phillies pitcher had the most hits during the 1993 season?
A. Curt Schilling
B. Terry Mulholland
C. Danny Jackson
D. Tommy Greene
Answer on page 76.

54. How many strikeouts did Cole Hamels get in Game One of the 2008 World Series?
A. 9
B. 7
C. 5
D. 11
Answer on page 76.

55. Game Five of the 2008 World Series is the only game in World Series history to be suspended. However, there were three tied World Series games (1907, 1912, 1922) that were all called due to the same problem. What was the problem?
A. Rain
B. Darkness
C. Lightning
D. Frost/snow
Answer on page 76.

56. Before Harry Kalas's decades-long "Outta here!" home-run call with the Phillies, he was part of the Houston Astros inaugural broadcast team at the Astrodome in 1965. What was his short-lived home-run call with Houston?
A. "That ball's in Astro orbit!"
B. "It's an Astro smash!"
C. "Houston, we have liftoff!"
D. "That ball's way out in the Astro-sphere!"
Answer on page 76.

57. Which Phillie inspired Harry Kalas's "Outta here!" home-run call?

A. Greg Luzinski
B. Tim McCarver
C. Steve Carlton
D. Larry Bowa

Answer on page 76.

58. Which minor-league team gave Harry Kalas his start in broadcasting in 1961?

A. Reading Phillies
B. Durham Bulls
C. Amarillo Sonics
D. Hawaii Islanders

Answer on page 76.

59. Who became the first pitcher to win the Cy Young Award in his first season with the Phillies?

A. Zack Wheeler
B. Roy Halladay
C. Steve Carlton
D. Steve Bedrosian

Answer on page 76.

60. In 2011, the Phillies sent Roy Halladay, Cole Hamels, and another starting pitcher to the All-Star Game. Who was the third pitcher?

A. Roy Oswalt
B. Vance Worley
C. Kyle Kendrick
D. Cliff Lee

Answer on page 76.

61. Who holds the Phillies' team record for most wins?
A. Roy Halladay
B. Steve Carlton
C. Cole Hamels
D. Grover Cleveland Alexander
Answer on page 76.

62. Who pitched the most innings in team history?
A. Cole Hamels
B. Grover Alexander
C. Curt Simmons
D. Robin Roberts
Answer on page 76.

63. Who has the best strikeout-to-walk ratio in team history?
A. Zack Wheeler
B. Curt Schilling
C. Cole Hamels
D. Cliff Lee
Answer on page 76.

64. Who holds the team record for most saves?
A. Brad Lidge
B. Tug McGraw
C. Jonathan Papelbon
D. Mitch Williams
Answer on page 76.

65. Despite the Phillies finishing with a record of 59–97 in 1972, Steve Carlton pitched a Cy Young Award–winning season completing it with how many wins?

A. 18
B. 20
C. 24
D. 27

Answer on page 77.

66. Who is the only Phillies pitcher to strike out 300+ batters in back-to-back seasons?

A. Steve Carlton
B. Jim Bunning
C. Curt Schilling
D. Grover Cleveland Alexander

Answer on page 77.

67. Who holds the team record for the lowest ERA in a single season?

A. Roy Halladay
B. Steve Carlton
C. Curt Schilling
D. Grover Cleveland Alexander

Answer on page 77.

68. Which one of these Phillies pitchers has not thrown an immaculate inning (three strikeouts on nine pitches)?

A. Juan Pérez
B. Andy Ashby
C. Cole Hamels
D. Robin Roberts
E. Roy Halladay

Answer on page 77.

69. How many Phils in history were named Phil?

A. 2
B. 9
C. 16
D. 23

Answer on page 77.

70. On June 23, 1971, which Phillies pitcher managed to throw a no-hitter while also hitting not one, but two home runs?

A. Steve Carlton
B. Rick Wise
C. Larry Christenson
D. Dick Ruthven

Answer on page 77.

71. Rick Wise was famously handy with the bat, hitting the most home runs by a pitcher in club history. Who shares the title with him?

A. Robert Person
B. Larry Christenson
C. Steve Carlton
D. Schoolboy Rowe

Answer on page 77.

72. Which unfortunate National League first did the Phillies find themselves on the wrong side of?

A. Unassisted triple play
B. No-hitter
C. Perfect game
D. Four-home-run game

Answer on page 77.

73. According to their officially listed weight, who is the heaviest pitcher to squeeze on a Phillies uniform?

A. Carlos Estévez
B. Aaron Harang
C. Elvis Araújo
D. Carlos Silva

Answer on page 77.

74. Who was the heaviest hitter?

A. Ryan Howard
B. Cameron Rupp
C. Rod Barajas
D. Justin Bour

Answer on page 77.

75. Who currently has the most career strikeouts per 9 IP in Phillies history?

A. Cliff Lee
B. Curt Schilling
C. Steve Carlton
D. Zack Wheeler

Answer on page 77.

76. Which of these Phillies pitchers has never hit a home run?

A. Joe Blanton
B. Cliff Lee
C. Aaron Nola
D. Steve Carlton

Answer on page 77.

77. Which starting pitcher from the 1993 Phillies was an All-Star that year?
A. Curt Schilling
B. Tommy Greene
C. Terry Mulholland
D. Ben Rivera
Answer on page 77.

78. How many Cy Young Awards did Hall of Famer Steve Carlton win throughout his career?
A. 2
B. 5
C. 3
D. 4
Answer on page 78.

79. In 2010, Roy Halladay threw a perfect game during the regular season and later went on to throw a no-hitter in his first career postseason start. What two teams did Doc perfect excellence against in 2010?
A. Marlins and Cubs
B. Braves and Mets
C. Reds and Dodgers
D. Marlins and Reds
Answer on page 78.

80. Who was the only pitcher on the 1993 Phillies team to hit double digits and lead the team in strikeouts in that postseason?
A. Terry Mulholland
B. Mitch Williams
C. Curt Schilling
D. Danny Jackson
Answer on page 78.

81. During the 2008 season, Brad Lidge went a perfect 41-for-41 in save opportunities during the regular season. How many saves did he secure during the 2008 postseason?
A. 4
B. 5
C. 6
D. 7
Answer on page 78.

82. How young was the youngest Phillie in team history?
A. 16
B. 17
C. 18
D. 19
Answer on page 78.

83. How old was the oldest Phillie in team history?
A. 44
B. 45
C. 46
D. 47
Answer on page 78.

84. There have been a total of nine relief pitchers to ever win the Cy Young Award. Which Phillies closer is among them?
A. Tug McGraw
B. Gene Garber
C. Steve Bedrosian
D. José Mesa
Answer on page 78.

85. How many times did Steve Carlton collect 20+ wins in a single season?

A. 2
B. 6
C. 4
D. 3

Answer on page 78.

86. Before being traded to the Texas Rangers at the deadline in 2015, Cole Hamels made one last start against the Chicago Cubs. What feat did Hamels accomplish in his final start with the Phillies?

A. He was ejected for hitting multiple batters
B. He pitched an immaculate inning
C. He pitched a no-hitter
D. He hit a home run

Answer on page 78.

87. Who was the pitcher on the mound when the Phillies clinched the 2007 National League East Division title?

A. Freddy Garcia
B. Ryan Madson
C. Tom Gordon
D. Brett Myers

Answer on page 78.

88. How many wins did Cole Hamels earn throughout his nine seasons with the Phillies?

A. 101
B. 114
C. 146
D. 162

Answer on page 79.

89. Who lead the Phillies in strikeouts during the decade from 2000–09?
A. Randy Wolf
B. Kevin Millwood
C. Brett Myers
D. Jamie Moyer
Answer on page 79.

90. On September 1, 2014, the Phillies threw a combined no-hitter against the Braves to win, 7–0. How many Phillies pitchers contributed to the historic feat?
A. 3
B. 4
C. 5
D. 6
Answer on page 79.

91. Out of the 12 no-hitters that Phillies pitchers have thrown throughout their history, there is only one team that they have no-hit multiple times. Which team is it?
A. New York Mets
B. San Francisco Giants
C. Houston Astros
D. Pittsburgh Pirates
Answer on page 79.

92. Which Phillies pitcher from 1990–present holds the team record for WAR for pitchers?
A. Cliff Lee
B. Cole Hamels
C. Roy Halladay
D. Curt Schilling
Answer on page 79.

93. During the 2023 Postseason, Zack Wheeler dominated the opposition going 3-0 in four starts and one relief appearance. What was his ERA for that stretch?
A. 1.50 ERA
B. 2.44 ERA
C. 1.95 ERA
D. 2.64 ERA
Answer on page 79.

94. In a 19-inning bout against the Cincinnati Reds in 2011, which Phillies infielder pitched in relief to secure the win?
A. Maikel Franco
B. Pete Orr
C. Plácido Polanco
D. Wilson Valdez
Answer on page 79.

95. On what holiday did Jim Bunning throw a perfect game back in 1964?
A. Mother's Day
B. Labor Day
C. Father's Day
D. Independence Day
Answer on page 79.

96. Who holds the all-time record for most home runs allowed in a single season?
A. Aaron Nola
B. Brett Myers
C. Chad Ogea
D. Robin Roberts
Answer on page 79.

97. Greg Gross had a franchise-record 117 hits as a pinch-hitter, but only a .298 slugging percentage. Who holds the Phillies record for slugging as a pinch-hitter?

A. Greg Dobbs
B. Jason Michaels
C. Matt Stairs
D. John Mayberry Jr.

Answer on page 79.

98. Who holds the lowest career WHIP in team history (walks + hits per inning pitched; min. 500 IP)?

A. Cliff Lee
B. Jim Bunning
C. George McQuillan
D. Zack Wheeler

Answer on page 79.

99. Who pitched the most shutouts in club history?

A. Grover Cleveland Alexander
B. Robin Roberts
C. Jim Bunning
D. Steve Carlton

Answer on page 80.

GENERAL ADMISSION

ANSWERS

1. A—Billy Hamilton. Hamilton has a .360 career batting average.

2. C—Chuck Klein. With a .553 slugging percentage, he has the highest in franchise history.

3. B—Mike Schmidt. The Hall of Famer scored a total of 1,506 runs for the Phils.

4. D—Ed Delahanty. With 158, Delahanty has the most triples all-time.

5. C—Chase Utley. Never one to shy away from a pitch, his 173 is the most by a Phillies player.

6. B—Pedro Feliz. Feliz knocked in Eric Bruntlett, who was pinch-running for Pat Burrell.

7. A—Josh Phelps. Born in Anchorage, Phelps went to high school in Idaho.

8. B—Rhéal Cormier. Cormier had a 3.7 WAR with Philadelphia, and no other Canadian came close.

9. D—Sid Fernandez. An alum of Kaiser High School in Honolulu, Sid pitched serviceably, yet briefly, for Philadelphia (9–7, 3.38 ERA in 22 starts).

10. D—Vicente Padilla. Padilla was famously part of the four-man haul the Phillies received from Arizona in exchange for Curt Schilling in 2000. He had a decent 14-year career that included a 3.98 ERA in 162 games with Philly.

11. D—1978. On April 28, 1978, the Phanatic made his debut.

12. B—Miss Piggy. Erickson designed Muppets Miss Piggy and Statler and Waldorf, and was responsible with creating other mascots, like Youppi! and Big Shot.

13. A—Baseball. Tubby Raymond would go on to a legendary career leading the University of Delaware's football team (1966–2001), but his head coaching duties began as the skipper of Maine's baseball program.

14. C—The San Diego Chicken. The San Diego Chicken's wild, brash antics inspired the Phillies to invent a more family-friendly version.

15. C—Tommy Lasorda. Lasorda chased the Phanatic and threw him to the ground down the left-field line. He admitted after the fact that the two were on good terms usually, but on that occasion, felt he "went a little too far."

16. D—*Sports Illustrated for Kids*. *SIFK* crowned the green giant "best ever," while Forbes named him "the best mascot in sports" in a 2008 issue.

17. A—The Galapagos Islands. Per Tom Burgoyne, who currently dons the suit, the Phanatic left the Galapagos in 1978 to pursue his dream in baseball.

18. A (The Phillie Phanatic), D (Youppi!), and E (The San Diego Chicken).

19. B—Ryan Howard. Howard averaged 10 home runs per at-bat in 2006. He is also third on the list with 11.3 in 2007.

20. C—Kyle Schwarber. Schwarber has a career mark of 12.5 HRs per AB, with Jim Thome second in the category at 13.3.

21. A—53. Never finished with 53 wins, and topped out at 60, 70, and 93 wins exactly once.

22. D—Thrice. That would be in 1979, 1983, and 1989. One Phillie played in all 163 in 1979 . . . but more on that later.

23. B—111. That was way back in 1941. Amazingly, they finished with two fewer losses the following season but actually did WORSE, dropping from a .279 win percentage to .278 in 1942.

24. B—Mickey Morandini. Mick turned the trick in 1992 against Pittsburgh.

25. A—Billy Maharg. Standing 5-foot-4, Maharg wasn't really a ballplayer. He was a pro boxer, had mob ties, was a 1919 Black Sox whistleblower, and made it into two separate MLB games on special circumstances. Also, his last name was GRAHAM backward . . . which probably means something bad.

26. A—Michael Schwimer. Schwimer (2011–12) is actually tied with Gene Conley (1959–60) at 6-foot-8.

27. A—1. Shared by three kings, Emil Gross, Bill McClellan, and Blondie Purcell in 1883.

28. C—Casey Stengel. Stengel played for the Phils in 1921, alongside another would-be Hall of Fame skipper— future NFL head coaching great, Greasy Neale. Later, Sparky Anderson played his only season in the bigs in 1959, with Philadelphia. Lasorda was born in Norristown and owned a restaurant with his brothers in Exton, but never played or managed outside of the

Dodgers organization. John Madden was drafted by the Eagles, but that's hardly relevant here.

29. D—Eddie Sawyer. Sawyer led the pennant-winning 1950 Whiz Kids, retired in 1953, then returned to manage the Phils from 1958–61.

30. C—2010. The hype around Roy Halladay's first season in Philadelphia brought out the phaithful in droves (3,777,322). Despite the club's recent success, the top five attendance totals all occurred from 2008 to 2012.

31. D—Pete Rose. Charlie Hustle played 'em all (+1) in 1979.

32. B—13. Thirteen top overall picks have played for the Phils since the first draft took place in 1965.

33. B—5. Alan Bannister, Dick Ruthven, Mark Davis, Pat Burrell, and Mickey Moniak.

34. A—Ryan Howard. Howard clubbed as many grand slams as Schmidt, Schwarber, and Harper combined (15; 5 apiece).

35. C—Gary Matthews. Matthews's OPS of 1.107 is the highest, but Harper is not far behind, at 1.090.

36. C—Ranger Suarez. Suarez has a minuscule 1.48 ERA in postseason play. However, Wheeler does hold the team record for postseason WHIP (walks + hits per IP) at 0.73.

37. C—Don Carman. None of the four ever got an XBH with the Phillies, but Carman had the most at-bats with 204.

38. C—48. *Yikes.*

39. D—Brett Myers. Myers fell just short, with 986 Ks with the Phillies.

40. C—José Mesa. Mesa accomplished this feat in 2001 (42 saves) and 2002 (45 saves).

41. D—Kent Tekulve. Tekulve pitched in 90 games in 1987, going 6–4 with a 3.09 ERA. He is one of just five pitchers to ever accomplish this feat in league history, and one of two to do so more than once (doing so three times, along with Mike Marshall).

42. E—Grover Cleveland Alexander. Alexander threw 16 shutouts in 1916.

43. B—Eric Milton. Milton led the league in homers allowed that season, but was the "ace" of the staff at 14–6 with a 4.75 ERA.

44. B—2021. Throwing a total of 1,480 strikeouts.

45. C—Steve Carlton. Lefty was "effectively wild," with 120 wild pitches.

46. C—214. As per a previous question, Eric Milton led the staff, and league, in homers allowed.

47. C—J. C. Romero. J. C. unlocked God Mode that playoffs (7.1 IP, 2 H, 0 ER, 7K, 3 BB).

48. C—Cole Hamels. Hamels led the team in 2008 with 196 Ks.

49. C—Corey Knebel. While the team had 42 total saves, Knebel led the team with a measly 12.

50. A—Joe Blanton. Surprised? His 195.1 IP were all but forgotten once the Phils started collecting aces.

51. C—Cliff Lee. In 40.1 innings (including two complete games), Lee struck out 33 during the 2009 postseason.

52. D—Curt Schilling. Not his best statistical season on paper, but 186 Ks was still a hefty number.

53. D—Tommy Greene. Greene could rake, racking up 16 hits in his '93 campaign.

54. C—Five. It was a terrific performance for Cole: 7 IP, 5 H, 2 ER, 5 K, 2 BB.

55. B—Darkness. The first World Series game played under lights was at Ebbets Field in 1949.

56. A—"That ball's in Astro orbit!" Kalas called orbit shots in Houston until joining the Phillies' broadcast team in 1971.

57. D—Larry Bowa. Bowa remarked during batting practice that one of Luzinski's bombs was "way outta here," and Kalas adopted the line for good.

58. D—Hawaii Islanders. After graduating from the University of Iowa in 1959, Kalas was drafted to the Army and stationed in Hawaii until 1961.

59. B—Roy Halladay. Doc entered the NL strong in 2010 (21–10, 2.44 ERA, 219 Ks).

60. D—Cliff Lee. Third ace in the deck!

61. B—Steve Carlton. Left has the most, with 241.

62. D—Robin Roberts. That would be the Hall of Famer, with 3,739.1 IP.

63. D—Cliff Lee. Lee's 6.556 K–W ratio is the highest in team history.

64. C—Jonathan Papelbon. The much-maligned closer had 123 saves in a Phillies uniform.

65. D—27. Carlton went 27–10 with a 1.97 ERA while throwing 30 complete games and striking out 310 batters.

66. C—Curt Schilling. He did so in 1997 (319) and 1998 (300).

67. D—Grover Cleveland Alexander. In 1915, Alexander had a 1.22 ERA in 376.1 IP.

68. E—Roy Halladay. Doc did just about everything else in a single game, but was never immaculate.

69. B—9. Nine Phils named Phil. Ten, if you count Phillippe Aumont. Phil Collins played the most seasons with Philadelphia (7; 1929–35).

70. B—Rick Wise. Wise threw a no-hitter and hit two home runs with three RBIs in a 4–0 win over Cincinnati.

71. B—Larry Christenson. Christenson and Wise each hit 11, but Wise used 58 fewer plate appearances to get there.

72. A—Unassisted triple play. The first unassisted TP in league history was completed by Ernie Padgett of the Braves in 1923. Phillies first baseman Walter Holke was the batter.

73. D—Carlos Silva. Silva tipped the scales at 280. Officially.

74. D—Justin Bour. Credit to Bour, 270 pounds listed, for being the only hitter other than Rupp (265) willing to admit they weigh over 250 pounds.

75. D—Zack Wheeler. With 10.057, Wheeler has the highest K per nine IP in Phils history.

76. C—Aaron Nola. Nola has never, and probably will never.

77. C—Terry Mulholland. Mulholland only made one All-Star Game.

78. D—4. Steve Carlton collected a total of four Cy Young Awards in his career—all with the Phils! He won in 1972, 1977, 1980, and 1982.

79. D—Marlins and Reds. On May 29, Roy Halladay threw a perfect game against the Florida Marlins in Miami. On October 6, 2010, Halladay no-hit the Cincinnati Reds in Game One of the NLDS. It was Halladay's first career postseason start.

80. C—Curt Schilling. Four GS, 31.1 IP, 28 Ks.

81. D—7. Brad Lidge went 7-for-7 in saves opportunities to secure the Phillies' second ever World Series Championship.

82. B—17. At seventeen years of age, Mike Loan, a Philly native, played in one game for the Phillies in 1912. He's one of 62 Phillies with a lifetime .500+ batting average with the club (min. two at-bats).

83. Trick question! Jamie Moyer owns the record with his age forty-seven season. But, he also had the record at ages forty-four, forty-five, and forty-six!

84. C—Steve Bedrosian. Bedrosian recorded 40 saves in 65 appearances, beating out Rick Sutcliffe to become the first and only Phillies closer to win a Cy Young Award.

85. C—4. Carlton accomplished this feat in 1972 (27–10), 1977 (23–10), 1980 (24–9), and 1982 (23–11).

86. C—He pitched a no-hitter. Hamels threw a no-hitter against the Cubs in his last Phillies start. Hamels struck out 13 while walking two, ending his career with the Phillies on an ultimate high.

87. D—Brett Myers. Myers struck out Wily Mo Peña of the Nationals to end the game and clinch the East.

88. B—114. Hamels is sixth all-time in franchise wins.

89. C—Brett Myers. Myers, a flashy starter and closer for the Phillies, racked up 986 Ks.

90. B—4. Cole Hamels, Jake Diekman, Ken Giles, and Jonathan Papelbon all combined to no-hit the Braves.

91. B—San Francisco Giants. Happened twice: Terry Mulholland on August 15, 1990; and Kevin Millwood, on April 27, 2003.

92. B—Cole Hamels. Hamels holds it, with a 42.0 (according to Baseball-Reference.com).

93. C—1.95 ERA. Wheeler walked just three batters in five starts that postseason.

94. D—Wilson Valdez. Valdez came into the game in the top of the 19th, throwing a scoreless inning and securing a win after a walk-off in the bottom of the 19th.

95. C—Father's Day. Jim Bunning no-hit the New York Mets in game one of a doubleheader on Father's Day, June 21, 1964.

96. D—Robin Roberts. In 1956, Roberts allowed 46 home runs . . . and that's not a typo. It was his third of four straight seasons leading the league in homers allowed. Roberts holds four of the top five seasons in that category.

97. D—John Mayberry Jr. After his first three years with the club, and 369 total plate appearances to begin his MLB career, Mayberry had amassed 21 home runs and an .846 OPS. His career tailed off after that, but he still holds the franchise record for slugging percentage as a pinch hitter, at .505.

98. D—Zack Wheeler. As of 2025, Wheeler is the Phillies WHIP leader, at 1.016. Three other members of the Phillies'

2025 starting rotation all finished the season in the top 35 in the category (Aaron Nola 11th, Christopher Sánchez 13th, Ranger Suarez 35th).

99. A—Grover Cleveland Alexander. GCA had a total of 61—more than Robin Roberts and Jim Bunning combined (35 and 23, respectively).

MODERN ERA (1900–PRESENT DAY)

QUESTIONS

The Modern Era represents a more structured version of Major League Baseball. For Pete Wood's sake, for much of the 1800s, players didn't have to wear gloves. These questions cover the civilized era of modern Phillies history.

1. Which Phillie has the highest single-season batting average?
A. Lefty O'Doul
B. Chuck Klein
C. Harry Walker
D. Richie Ashburn
Answer on page 87.

2. Which Phillie has the highest single-season slugging percentage?
A. Chuck Klein
B. Ryan Howard
C. Mike Schmidt
D. Dick Allen
Answer on page 87.

3. Which Phillie has the highest single-season on-base percentage?
   A. Roy Thomas
   B. Lefty O'Doul
   C. Bobby Abreu
   D. Mike Schmidt
   Answer on page 87.

4. Jimmy Rollins (778 in 2007; 758 in 2006) and Dave Cash (766 in 1975; 745 in 1974) each have two of the top five single-season plate appearance totals. Who is the other Phillie in the top five, with a second-best 773 total?
   A. Pete Rose
   B. Juan Samuel
   C. Richie Ashburn
   D. Lenny Dykstra
   Answer on page 87.

5. Who is the only player in team history to strike out 200 times? He did it twice . . .
   A. Jim Thome
   B. Kyle Schwarber
   C. Ryan Howard
   D. Mike Schmidt
   Answer on page 87.

6. Who is the Phillies' single-season walks leader?
   A. Lenny Dykstra
   B. Bobby Abreu
   C. Mike Schmidt
   D. Von Hayes
   Answer on page 87.

7. Who holds the single-season stolen-base mark with 72—17, more than anyone else in team history?
A. Sherry Magee
B. Jimmy Rollins
C. Hans Lobert
D. Juan Samuel
Answer on page 87.

8. Who holds the franchise record for extra-base hits in a season?
A. Jimmy Rollins
B. Ryan Howard
C. Bryce Harper
D. Chuck Klein
Answer on page 87.

9. According to Baseball-Reference.com, who holds the team record for adjusted career OPS+ (on-base percentage plus slugging percentage, adjusted for league and ballpark factors)?
A. Dick Allen
B. Gavy Cravath
C. Ed Delahanty
D. Bryce Harper
Answer on page 88.

10. Which slugger holds the Phils' single-season record for singles?
A. Richie Ashburn
B. Lefty O'Doul
C. Billy Hamilton
D. Doug Glanville
Answer on page 88.

11. Mike Schmidt of course leads most of the major run-producing stats in Phillies history, but who is second in RBIs?

A. Chuck Klein
B. Del Ennis
C. Jimmy Rollins
D. Ryan Howard

Answer on page 88.

12. Righthander Mike Schmidt, again, famously leads the franchise in career home runs (548), and it's probably easy to surmise from there that Ryan Howard leads the team from the opposite side of the plate. Who is second to each player?

Righty:

A. Pat Burrell
B. Del Ennis
C. Greg Luzinski
D. Dick Allen

Lefty:

A. Chase Utley
B. Chuck Klein
C. Bryce Harper
D. Kyle Schwarber

Answer on page 88.

13. Who has the highest single-season OPS mark (on-base + slugging)?

A. Lefty O'Doul
B. Ryan Howard
C. Mike Schmidt
D. Chuck Klein

Answer on page 88.

14. Who was intentionally walked the most times in one season?
A. Ron Northey
B. Ryan Howard
C. Mike Schmidt
D. Jim Thome
Answer on page 88.

15. Which Modern ERA MLB first happened against the Phillies?
A. Immaculate inning (three strikeouts on nine pitches)
B. No-hitter
C. Perfect game
D. Four-home-run game
E. Hit for the cycle
Answer on page 88.

16. Three players in team history have had qualified seasons with a 100 percent stolen-base success rate. Of the three, who stole the most bases?
A. Roman Quinn
B. Trea Turner
C. Chase Utley
Answer on page 89.

17. Who hit the fewest amount of home runs in their Phillies career (min. 1,500 at-bats)?
A. Rubén Amaro Sr.
B. Rubén Amaro Jr.
C. Greg Gross
D. Steve Jeltz
Answer on page 89.

18. Which pitcher has the highest career batting average in team history (min. 300 plate appearances)?

A. Schoolboy Rowe
B. Steve Carlton
C. Rick Wise
D. Tommy Greene

Answer on page 89.

19. Which pitcher hit the most batters in his Phillies career?

A. Steve Carlton
B. Jim Bunning
C. Kyle Kendrick
D. Aaron Nola

Answer on page 89.

20. Only five primary starters—pitchers who started at least 75 percent of all games played—have recorded five or more saves. Of the five, who had the most?

A. Grover Cleveland Alexander
B. Eppa Rixey
C. Robin Roberts
D. Dennis Bennett
E. Brett Myers

Answer on page 89.

MODERN ERA (1900–PRESENT DAY)

ANSWERS

1. A—Lefty O'Doul. Hit .389 in 1929.

2. A—Chuck Klein. Had a .687 slugging percentage in 1930.

3. B—Lefty O'Doul. Lefty at it again! Along with this .389 average, he also had a .465 on-base percentage in 1929.

4. D—Lenny Dykstra. With 773, Nails is just behind Rollins and Cash.

5. B—Kyle Schwarber. Not the most illustrious club to be a member, Schwarber hit the mark in back-to-back seasons: 2022 (200) and 2023 (215). He did, however, hit 46 and 47 home runs, respectively, along with 126 walks in 2023.

6. A—Lenny Dykstra. Nails at it again, with 129 walks in 1993.

7. D—Juan Samuel. Since 1900, only two players have had more than 50 stolen bases in a season. Sherry Magee had 55 in 1906, but Samuel has done it twice, swipping 53 in 1985 and 72 in 1984.

8. D—Chuck Klein. In 1930, Klein had 107 XBH. He is also second (103 in 1932) and third (94 in 1929) on the list. Baker Bowl was a helluva park!

9. Trick question! It is both A and B . . . and sometimes C. Allen, Cravath, and Delahanty all have a franchise-leading career OPS+ of 153, but this section is Modern Era only, so 11 of Ed's 13 seasons with Philadelphia would not qualify.

10. Another trick question! It is both A and B . . . and sometimes C. All three players hit 181 singles in a season (1951, 1929, 1894, respectively), but only Whitey and Lefty accomplished this during baseball's Modern Era.

11. D—Ryan Howard. With 1194, Howard is second all-time in the Modern Era.

12. Righty: B—Del Ennis. Lefty: A—Chase Utley. With 259, Ennis as the most behind Schmidt for righties. Utley clubbed 233 from the left side of the plate, but depending on when you're reading this, Harper and/or Schwarber may have caught up. Google it.

13. D—Chuck Klein. Also in 1930, Klein had a 1.123 OPS. Amazingly, he finished fourth in MVP voting, which would make you wonder how that was the case. Well, the winner was the Cubs' Hack Wilson (who had 56 HRs and 191 RBIs), second was the Cardinals' Frankie Frisch (.345/10/114), and third was Giant Bill Terry (.401 BA, 254 hits).

14. B—Ryan Howard. With 37 intentional walks in 2006, Howard holds the team record. Who's second? Well, it's Ryan Howard, with 35 in 2007.

15. B—No-hitter. Reds star Noodles Hahn no-hit the Phillies in 1900. Funny enough, the first Modern Era immaculate inning (Rube Waddell), perfect game (Cy Young), and four-home-run game (Lou Gehrig) all featured a Philadelphia team—the Athletics. The first cycle? That was Fred Clarke of the Pirates . . . but the first American League cycle came from Napoléon Lajoie of the Philadelphia A's just seven days later.

16. B—Trea Turner. In 2023, Turner stole 30 bases without being caught.

17. C—Greg Gross. A utility player for 10 years in Philadelphia—1,080 games in total—Gross had just one home run.

18. A—Schoolboy Rowe. Arguably the Phillies' best pitcher in 1943 (14–8, 2.94 ERA), Rowe was also the club's only .300 hitter (.300 in 138 PA). For his career, he had a .252 batting average.

19. B—Jim Bunning. While Kyle Kendrick had the highest percentage of hit batters, plunking 56 in 1,138.2 innings, Bunning has the overall record with 72.

20. C—Robin Roberts. Roberts saved 24 games for the Fightins, although he never tallied more than four in a single season. Myers had a second-best 21, all from the 2007 season.

HALL OF FAME

QUESTIONS

All of these questions have connections to MLB's Hallowed Hall.

1. Which Phillies announcer shares a name with the club's first chronological Hall of Famer (started with the Phils in 1886)?
A. Larry Andersen
B. Tom McCarthy
C. Benjamin Davis
D. Gregg Murphy
Answer on page 97.

2. Who was the oldest eventual Hall of Famer to play at least one season with the Phillies?
A. Grover Cleveland Alexander
B. Jim Kaat
C. Steve Carlton
D. Tony Pérez
Answer on page 97.

3. Who was the youngest?
   A. Ed Delahanty
   B. Richie Ashburn
   C. Dick Allen
   D. Scott Rolen
   Answer on page 97.

4. How many non-US-born Phillies are in the Hall?
   A. 3
   B. 6
   C. 9
   D. 12
   Answer on page 97.

5. Which Phillies Hall of Famer played for the most franchises?
   A. Dan Brouthers
   B. Hugh Duffy
   C. Dick Allen
   D. Jim Thome
   Answer on page 97.

6. Which Phillies Hall of Famer played the least amount of games with the club?
   A. Hack Wilson
   B. Ferguson Jenkins
   C. Ryne Sandberg
   D. Pedro Martinez
   Answer on page 97.

7. Who was the first Phillie to be elected to the Hall?
A. Grover Cleveland Alexander
B. Eddie Collins
C. Napoléon Lajoie
D. Ed Delehanty
Answer on page 98.

8. The Chicago Cubs' famous double-play combination of "Tinker to Evers to Chance!" in the early 1900s was immortalized in a poem by Franklin P. Adams in 1910. Who was the only member of the Hall of Fame trio to play for the Phillies?
A. Joe Tinker
B. Johnny Evers
C. Frank Chance
Answer on page 98.

9. Which Phillie received the highest percentage of votes in their Hall induction?
A. Steve Carlton
B. Pedro Martinez
C. Joe Morgan
D. Mike Schmidt
Answer on page 98.

10. 75 percentage of the vote is required for enshrinement. Which Phillie snuck in by just two votes (334 of 443)?
A. Fergie Jenkins
B. Scott Rolen
C. Jimmy Foxx
D. Billy Wagner
Answer on page 98.

11. Who is the only Hall of Fame manager during baseball's modern era to have skippered the Phillies?
A. Sparky Anderson
B. Harry Wright
C. Bucky Harris
D. Hugh Duffy
Answer on page 98.

12. Who is the only Native American pitcher—and Phillies alum—to get elected to the Hall?
A. Zack Wheat
B. Jim Thorpe
C. Chief Bender
D. Ben Tincup
Answer on page 98.

13. What's the only position at which the Phillies have never featured a Hall of Famer?
A. Catcher
B. DH
C. Second base
D. Shortstop
Answer on page 98.

14. What percentage of Hall of Famers played for the Philadelphia Phillies?
A. 8.4 percent
B. 11.9 percent
C. 13.3 percent
D. 15.2 percent
Answer on page 98.

15. Who is the only MLB Hall of Famer to go to LaSalle University?

A. Ferguson Jenkins
B. Hugh Duffy
C. Eppa Rixey
D. Hughie Jennings

Answer on page 98.

HALL OF FAME

ANSWERS

1. B—Tom McCarthy. Outfielder Tom McCarthy was inducted into the Hall of Fame in 1946, and Tom McCarthy has been the play-by-play man for the Phillies since 2008.

2. A—Grover Cleveland Alexander. GCA was forty-three years old in his farewell tour in Philly, after a 12-year stint with Chicago and St. Louis.

3. A—Ed Delahanty. Delahanty was twenty years old when he debuted for the Phils in 1888. Ashburn, Allen, and Rolen debuted at twenty-one.

4. A—3. That would be Fergie Jenkins (Canada), Tony Pérez (Cuba), and Pedro Martinez (Dominican Republic).

5. A—Dan Brouthers. Brouthers shares the HOF record with Deacon White, 10 franchises. In the Modern Era, Thome played for the most (six).

6. A—Hack Wilson. In his 12-year career, Wilson played 850 games with the Cubs, 319 with the Brooklyn Dodgers, 172 with the New York Giants, and just seven with the Phillies.

7. C—Napoléon Lajoie. Lajoie started his career with the Phillies (1896–1900) and was elected in the second class of inductees in 1937.

8. B—Johnny Evers. Evers played in 56 games for the Phils in 1917.

9. D—Mike Schmidt. At the time of Schmidt's induction in 1995, he received more votes than any other position player in Major League Baseball history (444, 96.52 percent).

10. A—Fergie Jenkins. Shortly after being traded to the Chicago Cubs, Jenkins pitched six straight seasons with at least 20 wins. No one has matched the effort since.

11. C—Bucky Harris. Harris spent part of the 1943 season as Phillies manager, sandwiched between World Series–winning efforts helming the Nationals (1924) and Yankees (1947).

12. C—Chief Bender. A Philly legend for sure, Bender spent most of his career with the Athletics, though his final two full seasons were with the Phillies.

13. A—Catcher. The Phillies have never had a Hall of Famer play a single game at catcher for the franchise. Jim Thome is the team's only DH representative.

14. C—13.3 percent. Only 37 people, 13.3 percent of all Hall of Fame players, laced 'em up for the Phils.

15. D—Hughie Jennings. Jennings attended both Cornell University and what was then LaSalle College.

OPENING DAY

QUESTIONS

The most wonderful time of the year! All of these questions relate to some of Philadelphia's most famous first days.

1. Who played in the most Opening Day games?
A. Richie Ashburn
B. Jimmy Rollins
C. Mike Schmidt
D. Larry Bowa
Answer on page 105.

2. Which pitcher got the most Opening Day starts in team history?
A. Steve Carlton
B. Robin Roberts
C. Aaron Nola
D. Chris Short
Answer on page 105.

3. Which catcher got the most Opening Day starts in team history?
   A. Darren Daulton
   B. J. T. Realmuto
   C. Mike Lieberthal
   D. Carlos Ruiz
   Answer on page 105.

4. Are the Phillies above, below, or at exactly .500 in their Opening Day history?
   A. Above
   B. Below
   C. .500
   Answer on page 105.

5. Who has the most wins as an Opening Day pitcher?
   A. Steve Carlton
   B. Curt Schilling
   C. Robin Roberts
   D. Grover Cleveland Alexander
   Answer on page 105.

6. Who has the most losses as an Opening Day pitcher?
   A. Steve Carlton
   B. Curt Schilling
   C. Robin Roberts
   D. Grover Cleveland Alexander
   Answer on page 105.

7. Seven Phillies are tied for the most hits in an Opening Day game (four), but only his one also reached base with a walk:
A. Phil Collins
B. Cy Williams
C. Sherry Magee
D. Mike Goliat
Answer on page 105.

8. Who has the most total bases in a single game?
A. Chase Utley
B. Alec Bohm
C. Sherry Magee
D. Don Money
Answer on page 106.

9. Most runs scored in a single game?
A. Chase Utley
B. Cody Asche
C. Sherry Magee
D. David Bell
Answer on page 106.

10. Most strikeouts recorded in a single game?
A. Curt Schilling
B. Chris Short
C. Roy Halladay
D. Zack Wheeler
Answer on page 106.

11. Most innings pitched in a single game?

A. Curt Schilling
B. Chris Short
C. Steve Carlton
D. Grover Cleveland Alexander

Answer on page 106.

12. Who has the most home runs in an Opening Day career?

A. Chuck Klein
B. Scott Rolen
C. Jimmy Rollins
D. Mike Schmidt

Answer on page 106.

13. Highest career batting average on Opening Day (min. 30 plate appearances)?

A. Carlos Ruiz
B. Sherry Magee
C. Chase Utley
D. Von Hayes

Answer on page 106.

14. Most career RBIs on Opening Day?

A. Jimmy Rollins
B. Mike Schmidt
C. Chuck Klein
D. Granny Hamner

Answer on page 106.

15. Lowest career ERA on Opening Day (min. 20 IP)?
A. Roy Halladay
B. Curt Schilling
C. Chris Short
D. Grover Cleveland Alexander
Answer on page 106.

16. Most career strikeouts on Opening Day?
A. Curt Schilling
B. Steve Carlton
C. Robin Roberts
D. Aaron Nola
Answer on page 107.

17. Ricky Bottalico is tied for the most career saves for the Phillies on Opening Day. How many did he rack up?
A. 1
B. 2
C. 3
D. 4
Answer on page 107.

OPENING DAY

ANSWERS

1. C—Mike Schmidt. Naturally, it is Schmidt, with 16. Fun fact: the Phillies were just 3–13 on Opening Day with Schmitty in the lineup.

2. A—Steve Carlton. Again, no surprise. Carlton started 14 Opening Days, but Robin Roberts holds the record for consecutive Opening Day starts, with 12.

3. C—Mike Lieberthal. The two-time All-Star started in 10 Opening Days during his 13 seasons in Philly.

4. B—Below. Through the 2025 season, the Phillies have a 68–73–2 record (476). They were last at exactly .500 after a win over the Florida Marlins in 2002 (59–59–2).

5. C—Robin Roberts. In 12 career starts, Roberts went 5–6 with a 4.22 ERA, with eight complete games. Chris Short had the most Opening Day shutouts, with three.

6. A—Steve Carlton. In 14 starts, Carlton went 3–9 with a 4.30 ERA.

7. A—Phil Collins. This happened in 1932, and Collins was a *pitcher*. Incredible.

8. D—Don Money. In a 7–6 loss in 11 innings, Money collected 10 total bases on a double and two home runs, driving in five of Philly's six runs.

9. B—Cody Asche. With four runs, he is tied with 29 others for the Major League Opening Day lead. But alphabetically? Asche tops 'em all!

10. B—Chris Short. Short fanned 18 Mets during the last series of the 1965 season. He pitched 15 innings of shutout baseball and still didn't get the win! In fact, no one did; the game ended in a 0–0 tie. Art Mahaffey owns the Phillies nine-inning mark with 17 Ks in a 1961 win over the Chicago Cubs.

11. B—Chris Short. Short strikes again, as he pitched 9.2 innings in an Opening Day, 12-inning 3–2 win over the St. Louis Cardinals in 1966.

12. D—Mike Schmidt. Ho hum, another Phillies home-run record for Michael Jack. He clubbed five total, while Klein, Rolen, and Rollins are second in team history, with three each.

13. B—Sherry Magee. Magee batted .419 in nine Opening Day games. For what it's worth, Chooch has the career record since 1915, hitting .400 in eight games.

14. C—Chuck Klein. Klein's 11 RBIs on Opening Day edge out Rollins's 10.

15. A—Roy Halladay. Doc sported a 0.86 ERA on Opening Day in three Phillies starts. He's one of just five Phillies all-time with an Opening Day ERA below 4.00 (Schilling, Short, Alexander, and Terry Mulholland).

16. B—Steve Carlton. This was an easy one. Carlton has nearly as many Ks on Opening Day (66) as the next two pitchers on the list combined, Roberts and Nola (37, 35 respectively).

17. A—1. Ricky Bo shares the title with six other pitchers.

THE VET

QUESTIONS

Veterans Stadium: A concrete jungle where dreams, and many nightmares, were made.

1. Who had the first hit in Vet history?
A. Larry Bowa
B. Don Money
C. Willie Montañez
D. Deron Johnson
Answer on page 115.

2. Who had the final hit?
A. Marlon Byrd
B. Pat Burrell
C. Mike Lieberthal
D. Chase Utley
Answer on page 115.

3. Who had the first win?
A. Rick Wise
B. Jim Bunning
C. Bill Stoneman
D. Steve Renko
Answer on page 115.

4. Who had the last win?
   A. Kevin Millwood
   B. Randy Wolf
   C. Al Leiter
   D. Greg Maddux
   Answer on page 115.

5. Who hit the first home run?
   A. Larry Bowa
   B. Willie Montañez
   C. Don Money
   D. Deron Johnson
   Answer on page 115.

6. Who hit the last home run?
   A. Pat Burrell
   B. Bobby Abreu
   C. David Bell
   D. Jim Thome
   Answer on page 115.

7. Who hit the most homers in a single Vet season?
   A. Mike Schmidt
   B. Greg Luzinski
   C. Pat Burrell
   D. Jim Thome
   Answer on page 115.

8. The Phillies only had one season at the Vet with a total attendance over three million. Which season was it?
A. 1977
B. 1980
C. 1993
D. 2002
Answer on page 116.

9. Which season saw the most Phillies home runs at the Vet?
A. 1977
B. 1979
C. 1980
D. 1993
Answer on page 116.

10. Who helped the Phillie Phanatic press the ceremonial plunger to demolish the Vet on March 21, 2004?
A. Mike Schmidt
B. Greg Luzinski
C. Jimmy Rollins
D. Jim Thome
Answer on page 116.

11. Citizens Bank Park broke ground in 2002 and cost $458 million to build. How much did the Vet cost upon its completion in 1971?
A. $45 million
B. $55 million
C. $65 million
D. $75 million
Answer on page 116.

12. What was the original baseball capacity for Vet Stadium?
A. 50,371
B. 52,371
C. 54,371
D. 56,371
Answer on page 116.

13. In his book, *The Secret Apartment*, author Tom Garvey recounts his time living in a secret storage space at the Vet in the '80s. How long did he live there?
A. One year
B. Two years
C. Three years
D. Four years
Answer on page 116.

14. On June 25, 1971, the longest home run ever hit at the Vet landed in the right field 600 level, estimated at 458 feet. The spot where it landed was marked with an "S" for this star who slugged it:
A. Ron Santo
B. Willie Stargell
C. Rusty Staub
D. Mike Schmidt
Answer on page 116.

15. A Vet Stadium twinight doubleheader between the Phillies and San Diego Padres began on July 2, 1993, at 5:05 p.m. and, after multiple rain delays, concluded at 4:40 a.m. the following morning. With an estimated 6,000 fans still in attendance, this Phillie hit the walk-off game winner to take the second game and split the series:
A. John Kruk
B. Tommy Greene
C. Mitch Williams
D. Milt Thompson
Answer on page 116.

16. Two Phils no-hitters were tossed at the Vet, against the same team. Which?
A. Los Angeles Dodgers
B. Montreal Expos
C. San Diego Padres
D. San Francisco Giants
Answer on page 116.

17. How many times did the Phillies top three million in attendance in a single season at the Vet?
A. 1
B. 2
C. 3
D. 4
Answer on page 116.

18. What mode of transportation delivered the ceremonial first ball at the stadium's first official game in 1971?
A. Limousine
B. Skydiver
C. Helicopter
D. Motorcycle
Answer on page 116.

19. Which future Phillie got the first postseason base hit at the Vet?
A. Pete Rose
B. Tony Pérez
C. Joe Morgan
D. Rawly Eastwick
Answer on page 116.

20. At the Vet's opening in 1971, how much was the "Family Deal"—four each of hot dogs, sodas, and ice cream?
A. $3.00
B. $3.40
C. $4.00
D. $4.40
Answer on page 117.

21. What year was the first official proposal for Veterans Stadium?
A. 1954
B. 1957
C. 1960
D. 1963
Answer on page 117.

THE VET

ANSWERS

1. A—Larry Bowa. On April 10, 1971, Bowa led off the game for the Phillies, singling to right field off Expos starter Bill Stoneman for the first hit at the Vet.

2. B—Pat Burrell. Burrell singled in the bottom of the ninth of the Vet's final game, on September 28, 2003. Utley hit into a double play to end the game right after.

3. B—Jim Bunning. At thirty-nine years old, Bunning—the oldest starting pitcher in baseball—got the win for the Vet's inaugural game.

4. D—Greg Maddux. Maddux got the win at the last game at the Vet, a 5–2 Braves victory.

5. C—Don Money. Money hit the first Vet homer in the sixth inning of the inaugural game.

6. D—Jim Thome. The Hall of Famer Thome hit a solo shot in the eighth inning against Atlanta's Will Cunnane, on September 27, 2003.

7. D—Jim Thome. That would also be Thome, who clubbed a Vet record 28 dingers in 2003.

8. C—1993. The worst-to-first '93 season saw the ninth highest total attendance in team history.

9. A—1977. The Phillies clubbed 101 homers at home that season, winning 60 of their 81 games at the Vet.

10. B—Greg Luzinski.

11. A—$45 million. Adjusting for inflation, the $45 million was still less than half the Bank's cost in 2002 dollars ($213.4 million).

12. D—56,371. While the football capacity exceeded 65,000, the baseball was just over 56,000.

13. B—Two years. Garvey, a parking lot supervisor, hid out in the space from October 1979 to the end of 1981.

14. B—Willie Stargell. The "Stargell Star" remained until the stadium's demolition in 2004.

15. C—Mitch Williams. It was the last of three hits total in Williams's career. In fact, it raised his lifetime batting average from .133 to .188.

16. D—San Francisco Giants. Terry Mulholland no-hit the Giants on August 15, 1990, and Kevin Millwood turned the trick on April 27, 2003.

17. A—1. Happened just once, in the 1993 season. It was one of 12 attendance seasons over three million (3,137,674)—the others are all claimed by Citizens Bank Park.

18. C—Helicopter. The ball was dropped via helicopter and caught by bullpen coach Mike Ryan.

19. A—Pete Rose. Reds (and eventually Phillies) legend Charlie Hustle led off with a double in Game One of the 1976 NLCS.

20. D—$4.40. This is the equivalent of about $25 in 2026 buying power. At the time, fans complained because New York and Pittsburgh were charging just $3.60 for the same deal.

21. A—1954. Fairmount Park commissioner (and father of actress Grace Kelly) John B. Kelly Sr. first proposed the $10 million plan that would eventually balloon to $63 million in costs by the stadium's completion in early 1971.

THE BANK: BEGINNINGS

QUESTIONS

Citizens Bank Park's story is still being written, but do you know everything about the Bank's famous firsts?

1. Who had the first base hit at CBP?
A. Jimmy Rollins
B. D'Angelo Jimenez
C. Austin Kearns
D. Ryan Freel
Answer on page 127.

2. Who hit the first home run at CBP?
A. Bobby Abreu
B. Jim Thome
C. Pat Burrell
D. Ken Griffey Jr.
Answer on page 127.

3. Who nabbed the first stolen base?
A. Jimmy Rollins
B. Placido Polanco
C. Marlon Byrd
D. Barry Larkin
Answer on page 127.

4. Who was the first to strike out?
   A. Adam Dunn
   B. Barry Larkin
   C. Wily Mo Peña
   D. Ken Griffey Jr.
   Answer on page 127.

5. Randy Wolf was the first pitcher at the Bank—and got the first park's first single—but he did not secure the club's first win at their new digs. Who did?
   A. Rhéal Cormier
   B. Ryan Madson
   C. Eric Milton
   D. Brett Myers
   Answer on page 127.

6. Braves star Andruw Jones hit the first grand slam at the ballpark, but who hit the first one in the Phillies uniform?
   A. Jim Thome
   B. Pat Burrell
   C. Marlon Byrd
   D. Chase Utley
   Answer on page 127.

7. Who hit the first inside-the-park home run?
   A. Carlos Ruiz
   B. Placido Polanco
   C. Jimmy Rollins
   D. Chase Utley
   Answer on page 127.

8. Who hit for the first cycle at the Bank?
A. David Bell
B. Jimmy Rollins
C. Preston Wilson
D. José Vidro
Answer on page 128.

9. Who had the first three-home-run game?
A. Mike Lowell
B. Jim Thome
C. Ryan Howard
D. Juan Encarnación
Answer on page 128.

10. Who had the only four-home-run game?
A. Mike Cameron
B. Giancarlo Stanton
C. Kyle Schwarber
D. J. D. Martinez
Answer on page 128.

11. Who was the first interleague opponent at CBP?
A. Toronto Blue Jays
B. New York Yankees
C. Houston Astros
D. Minnesota Twins
Answer on page 128.

12. What year did the Bank surpass 3.5 million in attendance for the first time, setting a then-record for franchise attendance?
A. 2004
B. 2007
C. 2008
D. 2009
Answer on page 128.

13. What year did Citizens Bank Park have its first season with less than 1.5 million in attendance?
A. 2017
B. 2018
C. 2019
D. 2020
Answer on page 128.

14. The Phillies have fallen short of 800 runs scored for the past 16 seasons (2010–2025). How many runs did the club score in the first year at CBP?
A. 820
B. 830
C. 840
D. 850
Answer on page 128.

15. Who was the first manager with a sub-.500 record in the Citizens Bank Park era?
A. Larry Bowa
B. Charlie Manuel
C. Ryne Sandberg
D. Pete Mackanin
Answer on page 128.

16. According to Baseball-Reference, who was the first Phillie with a WAR of 9.0 or greater in the Citizens Bank Park era?

A. Roy Halladay
B. Chase Utley
C. Aaron Nola
D. Cliff Lee

Answer on page 128.

17. Which unlikely Phillie hit the first walk-off home run at CBP?

A. Todd Pratt
B. Doug Glanville
C. Tomás Pérez
D. Jason Michaels

Answer on page 128.

18. Who hit the first walk-off grand slam in CBP history?

A. John Mayberry
B. Marlon Byrd
C. Ryan Howard
D. Pat Burrell

Answer on page 129.

19. Who joined Hall of Famers Mike Schmidt, Steve Carlton, and Robin Roberts for the ceremonial first pitch at the Bank's inaugural game, on April 12, 2004?

A. Harry Kalas
B. Jim Bunning
C. Richie Ashburn
D. Larry Bowa

Answer on page 129.

20. Which Phillie was credited with the loss for the first ever postseason game at the Bank?

A. Jamie Moyer
B. Cole Hamels
C. Tom Gordon
D. Brett Myers

Answer on page 129.

21. Who got the first postseason hit in CBP history?

A. Garret Atkins
B. Todd Helton
C. Yorvit Torrealba
D. Troy Tulowitzki

Answer on page 129.

22. Who hit the first home run in the Bank's postseason history?

A. Matt Holliday
B. Troy Tulowitzki
C. Aaron Rowand
D. Pat Burrell

Answer on page 129.

23. For the first time in 2008, *Sports Illustrated* had fans rank all 30 MLB stadiums based on affordability, food, team quality, tradition, atmosphere, fan IQ, hospitality, promotions, traffic, and neighborhood. Where did Citizens Bank Park rank?

A. 8
B. 9
C. 10
D. 11

Answer on page 129.

24. Who was the first Phillie to take home a regular-season award in the Citizens Bank Park era?

A. Bobby Abreu
B. Chase Utley
C. Ryan Howard
D. Mike Lieberthal

Answer on page 129.

25. The first idea for (and of) Citizens Bank Park came from then-Phillies president Bill Giles in 1992. He visited another team's ballpark and immediately told ownership that Phillies fans deserved an intimate ballpark just like it. Which stadium was the first inspiration for the Bank?

A. Coors Field
B. Wrigley Field
C. Fenway Park
D. Camden Yards

Answer on page 129.

26. Which band/artist was the first to perform at Citizens Bank Park?

A. Billy Joel
B. Bruce Springsteen and the E Street Band
C. Jimmy Buffett and the Coral Reefer Band
D. Elton John

Answer on page 129.

27. On June 17, 2003, the Phillies inked the first corporate stadium-naming sponsorship in franchise history. When is the (potentially) last season for "Citizens Bank Park?"

A. 2028
B. 2033
C. 2038
D. 2043

Answer on page 130.

28. Who was the starting pitcher on Opening Day 2004 when the Phillies debuted Citizens Bank Park?

A. Randy Wolf
B. Eric Milton
C. Vicente Padilla
D. Gavin Floyd

Answer on page 130.

THE BANK: BEGINNINGS

ANSWERS

1. B—D'Angelo Jimenez. Jimenez is credited as the first batter, first to get a hit, and the first to get a double—all at once, against the Reds, on April 12, 2004.

2. A—Bobby Abreu. Abreu hit the first one out in the first inning. He is credited with the first run scored and first RBI.

3. C—Marlon Byrd. Byrd nabbed it in the third inning of the opening game. Interestingly enough, he would only have one more steal on the season, on April 23 in Montreal.

4. D—Ken Griffey Jr. was punched out in the first inning by Randy Wolf.

5. A—Rhéal Cormier. Cormier was credited with the club's first win of the season in the second game, over Pittsburgh. Six games later, he got the first ever win at CBP.

6. C—Marlon Byrd. Byrd hit the slam against Milwaukee on August 29.

7. C—Jimmy Rollins. On June 20, 2004, J-Roll touched 'em all against the Kansas City Royals.

8. A—David Bell. Bell completed one of roughly 350 cycles in MLB history, on June 28, 2004, against the Montreal Expos. He drove in six runs—a career high—in a 14–6 victory.

9. A—Mike Lowell. Lowell, then on the Marlins, had the first multi-homer game in CBP history, on April 21, 2004.

10. C—Kyle Schwarber. He hit four Schwarbombs on August 28, 2005, against the Atlanta Braves. It was the first (and through 2025 only) time in his career that he had belted four dingers in a game.

11. D—Minnesota Twins. The Twins lost to the Phils, 11–6, on June 11, 2004.

12. D—2009. The Phils followed their championship season with a then-franchise record 3,600,693 fans in 2009.

13. D—2020. Covid kept the gates closed; no fans allowed. It's hard to do worse than zero.

14. C—840. The Fightins scored 840 runs in 2003, the first of four straight seasons with 800 runs scored. Impressive considering they only have 13 such seasons in club history since 1900.

15. B—Charlie Manuel. Charlie didn't have a losing season with Philadlephia until his final season with the club (53–67). Sandberg took over midseason and finished 20–22.

16. B—Chase Utley. Utley was the first in 2008 (9.0), while Lee (9.0, 2011) and Nola (9.2, 2018) round out the trio of nines.

17. B—Doug Glanville. Glanville walked it off on April 18, 2004, against the Expos. It was the penultimate home run of his nine-year career (59 in total).

18. A—John Mayberry. Mayberry hit the grand walk-off on June 4, 2013, against the Marlins.

19. C—Richie Ashburn. Richard Ashburn, son of Phillies legend Richie, completed the foursome.

20. B—Cole Hamels. Hamels would be World Series MVP the following season, but he earned the first postseason L in the Phillies new ballpark in 2007. The Phils ended up getting swept by the Rockies in the NLDS.

21. B—Todd Helton. Helton tripled off Hamels in the second inning in Game One of the 2007 NLDS.

22. C—Aaron Rowand. This was a close one! Rowand hit the first postseason bomb at the Bank in the fifth inning of Game One of the 2007 NLDS. Burrell hit a homer of his own the very next at-bat.

23. C—10. The Phillies ranked 10th, though the list caught some guff with Wrigley Field (15th), Yankee Stadium (20th) and Fenway Park (21st) all falling outside of the top 10. Cleveland's Progressive Field took the top spot.

24. A—Bobby Abreu. He won a Silver Slugger in 2004. He got a Gold Glove the following season, while Ryan Howard won Rookie of the Year.

25. D—Camden Yards. The brainchild of Janet Marie Smith, 1992 was the first season for Camden Yards, and it's an obvious inspiration for the design of CBP.

26. C—Jimmy Buffett and the Coral Reefer Band. Mr. Margaritaville threw the first concert in 2005. There have been 46 concerts at the Bank through 2025.

27. A—2028. Ben Silver prognosticated in a 2022 *Sports Illustrated* article that the Phillies might call "Wawa Park" home in 2029.

28. A—Randy Wolf. A fan favorite, Wolf got the nod for the inaugural game.